Bathwick

Echoes of the Past

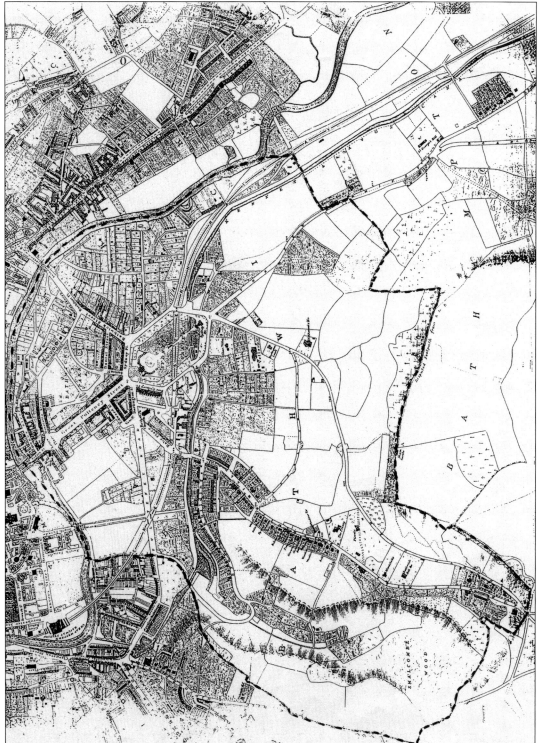

Fig. 1 Section from Cotterell's *Map of Bath*, 1852, showing the original boundaries of the Parish of Bathwick. (*Bath Record Office*)

Bathwick

Echoes of the Past

The Bathwick Local History Society

Cover illustrations:
(*front*) A section from *The South-east Prospect of the City of Bath*, Samuel and Nathaniel Buck, 1734. (*Bath Record Office*)
(*rear*) Not a hard hat in sight! Work on the steeple of St. John the Baptist Church by Frederick Hanks & Sons, c.1939. (*BLHS Archives*)

First published in 2008 by The Bathwick Local History Society in association with Millstream Books, Bath

Set in Palatino and Apple Chancery

Printed in Great Britain by The Short Run Press, Exeter

© The Bathwick Local History Society 2008

ISBN 978 0 948975 84 4

British Library Cataloguing-in-Publication Data:
a catalogue record for this book is available from the British Library

CONTENTS

INTRODUCTION *Michael Rowe*   6

BATHWICK – MANOR AND PARISH   7

THE PULTENEY PURCHASE   12

Sir William's Plan   14

Bathwick Quarries   17

Local Difficulties   20

Laying Out the 'New Town'   23

Planning for an Invasion   27

From Pulteney to Vane   28

Bathwick New Church   29

A Royal Visit   32

Bathwick Mews and Transport   34

Cleveland Bridge   37

THE RISE OF VICTORIAN BATHWICK

The New Era   39

The Canal Makes Way for the Railway   42

Lighting the Parish   44

St. Mary's by Gaslight   46

Smallcombe Vale Cemeteries   48

St. John the Baptist Church   52

Bathwick Schools   56

The Folly and Cremorne Gardens   62

The Boating Station   65

St. John's Road   67

Sham Castle Lane and Vellore Lane   70

Henrietta Park   72

A 'Home for Strays'   75

Local Traders Serving the Parish   76

Villa Fields and the Forester Estate   80

BUT WHAT WAS THE WEATHER LIKE?

The Years of the Floods   87

NOTES AND REFERENCES   93

APPENDIX – Bathwick street names associated with the Pulteney family or their successors   97

INDEX   98

ADDITIONAL BIBLIOGRAPHY   103

ACKNOWLEDGEMENTS   104

Note: In captions to the illustrations the abbreviation BLHS is used to represent The Bathwick Local History Society.

INTRODUCTION

Michael Rowe

The success of *Bathwick: A Forgotten Village* has confirmed the public appetite for approachable local history publications. The first book from The Bathwick Local History Society undoubtedly rekindled interest in life on the east bank of the river. It underlined the view that the successes and woes of enduring Bath families and of working people are just as fascinating as those of the grandees, who so often just come and go according to fashion.

This sequel explores other dimensions of the development of the whole area and gives insights into the early management of the parish. The misery of the poor, the horrors of epidemics and of the most severe floods Bath has ever known, add that pathos and reality to what otherwise could have descended into an account of bucolic village life.

There is an appreciation of the contribution of philanthropy to the struggles to provide places of worship, and the spats that arose in the pursuit of these high ideals.

Provision for the other way to lift the spirits appears in descriptions of long lost, and mainly forgotten, pleasure gardens and of the boating station.

The high aspirations of Sir William Pulteney left Bathwick with one of the finest streets in Europe. Yet we now hear something of the other effects of his development as seen from a local perspective.

Confusion often surrounds the subsequent ownership and management of Bathwick after the death of the last of the Pulteneys. Here, however, more is made clear. There is an understanding of the street names and there are pictures of the people who determined the way in which the face of the hillsides and floodplains would go on changing, when disciplined thinking still seemed to govern development. The latter years of one-family control, through an agent and estate architect, are revealed and allow a stark comparison with the 20th-century situation. Then, the estate largely was sold off into multiple ownership; piecemeal, architecturally inconsistent and incoherent infill developments commenced, and the character of Bathwick changed again. Description and analysis of that period is, however, left to others in the future.

The core researchers and authors remain the same as those for the very successful first book and, thus, there is an easy consistency in the style of writing and feel for the subject. As is the nature of The Bathwick Local History Society, other members have come forward freely with invaluable contributions and refreshing insights, which will also provoke the reader to ask for more.

BATHWICK – MANOR AND PARISH

From Anglo-Saxon times, England was divided into manors and parishes. Ecclesiastical in origin, parishes were the local unit of church government, each parish under the care of a parson or minister with 'permanent cure of souls'. Manors were the primary unit of civil administration in the country, varying enormously in size from a few acres to many square miles. Parish and manor were thus quite distinct, not necessarily with the same boundaries. Over the centuries the manor lost administrative power to the parish. By the 17th and 18th centuries, manorial government had largely fallen into decay. This left local affairs in the hands of parish institutions such as the vestry committee, while the manor came to mean simply a landed estate with tenants. Such was the manorial property which William Pulteney purchased in 1727.

In Bathwick, the manor and the parish always had the same boundaries:

> *it often happens that the parish boundaries divide the land into a series of roughly parallel bands extending from the river to the top of the hill.*[1]

At 600 acres the parish of Bathwick was quite small in comparison with its neighbours Bathampton (933 acres) and Lyncombe and Widcombe (1,843 acres).

Although we do not have any visible evidence of Saxons in Bathwick, this parish appears to be typical of many others that date from the 9th and 10th centuries.

The tiny 12th-century church of St. Mary's Bathwick was demolished in 1818[2] but surviving records date from 1668 and tell us something of the life of the parish before later developments changed it into the Bathwick we see today. Although now politically divided into wards by a system that gradually evolved from the creation of the civil parish in 1894, its original ecclesiastical boundaries remain largely unchanged.

After the dissolution of the monasteries in Tudor England, each parish became responsible for the relief of its poor, the enforcement of law and order, and care of its roads. Vestry committees were established. These governing bodies were made up of the Rector, the Parish Clerk, Churchwardens, Overseers of the Poor and Constables or Tythingmen whose duties included setting the church and poor rate and the management of parish accounts.

Parish meetings were held quarterly in the church vestry and at Easter the bell rang to summon the vestry committee to read and agree the accounts, appoint officers for the ensuing year and record the Minutes.

Apart from the Rector and his parish clerk, all the committee posts were untrained, unpaid and generally unpopular and it was often suggested that they [the posts] should go "from house to house in rotation for ever."[3]

The office of churchwarden dates back to the 14th century when any parishioner, male or female, could be nominated or compelled to stand for election for the role which was often difficult to carry out. Churchwardens kept the parish accounts and were open to prosecution if any impropriety were found. Although the post still exists within the church today, it is now a voluntary position and bears few comparisons with earlier times.

In 1638 the Glebe Terrier[4] for Bathwick recorded its land as

Imprimis the Parsonage house w'th a garden and an Aker of ground adjoyning to it. It's the barne and about ... lugge of ground belongeing to it.
It's one ground called Woodclose containing four Akers.

Fig. 2 Bathwick Street, August 2007. Demolition of the Bathwick Tyres premises and a petrol station. This plot of ground was once part of Woodclose. (*BLHS Archives*)

The 1664 Hearth Tax returns show a small village of just 12 dwellings, some with only one or two hearths and others with up to five hearths, these latter the homes, perhaps, of skilled craftsmen or small merchants and city shopkeepers. One building contained six hearths.[5] At this time the lower slopes of the land surrounding the village consisted mainly of orchards and meadows gently rising up towards common ground with hazel woods above. Many of the orchards were let and the produce sold in the city markets. Pieces of arable land were also let as pasture for grazing sheep.

By 1678 a (second) 'Burial in Wool' Act, intended to support the wool trade nationally, was passed. This Act decreed that

no corpse of any person (except those who shall die of the plague), shall be buried in any shirt, shift, sheet or shroud or anything whatsoever, made or mingled with flax, hemp, silk, hair, gold or silver, or in any other stuff or thing other than what is made of sheep's wool only ...

A relative of the deceased was required to swear an affidavit and a record made in the parish registers, by the parson, that such a burial had taken place. Penalties were harsh – a fine of £5 levied on the estate of the deceased and those connected with the burial.[6] It was possible, if wealthy, to pay the levy and the deceased to be "buried in linen" or some other material. The Rector of Bathwick at this time was the Reverend William Heath who held the Living for about 36 years, and parish records kept by him show those "buryed in woolen" and just one burial, "William Lewis Sen in Linnen", possibly indicating that life in this small hamlet was generally rather austere.

By 1721 the Rector of Bathwick was the Reverend Richard Huson. Many of our early records come from a ledger purchased by Thomas Batchelor, churchwarden in 1728, *by order of the Parson [the Reverend Huson] ... for the better keeping of an account of the Burials Christenings and Weddings ...*

In 1767 records portray Bathwick as a sparsely populated rural parish with a church rate of one penny in the pound. Other sources of revenue included the poor rate and burial fees. Paupers were buried at cost to the parish and from 1766 to 1768 over 30 people from the "Poore house in Bathe" including two women with smallpox were also interred here. Smallpox was endemic throughout the 18th and 19th centuries and in the Bath area over a 12-week period from 1st May to 27th July 1805 there were 60 authenticated deaths from the disease, 16 of these occurring in this parish. Later the fatal 'Asiatic' cholera was also present in the city for which the law required burial within 24 hours of death.

Prior to burial the Sanctus or tenor bell was tolled by the sexton and the number of strokes indicated male, female or child. This was then followed by a further stroke for each year of age.[7]

> *... it is ordered that no Corps that is not of this Parish shall be buried in the Churchyard in the Parish of Bathwick without paying one shilling for the use of the Black Cloth. If not agreeable to such persons as have a Corps to be buried to pay the one shilling, the Corps may be Interred without paying the above one shilling then they must not have the Bell to wring or Toll and also not be permitted to have the Corps to be carried into the Church.*

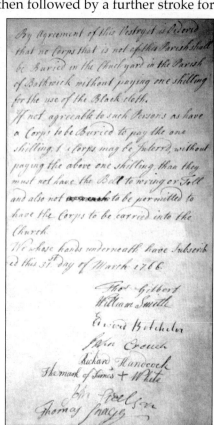

Fig. 3 (*left*) The tombstone of Daniel Palmer (1786-1839) in Old St. Mary's Churchyard, Henrietta Road. Daniel Palmer was sexton of the parish for about 30 years until he died. (*BLHS Archives*)

Fig. 4 (*right*) Bathwick Churchwardens Accounts Book 1766-1807; entry made on 31st March 1766. The 'Black Cloth' or Pall was used to drape a coffin. Reference here is to the one owned by the parish church of Bathwick. The payment of one shilling for its use was in addition to the burial fees payable to the Rector. Other fees payable to the parish included candles for lighting the church. (*Somerset Record Office, D/P/batw.m4/1/1*)

The churchwarden's accounts record a variety of disbursements including payments made to the local inn for bread and wine for sacramental use within the church. Villagers were paid for repairing and washing church vestments and small sums were also given out for trapping and killing small animals and birds – an early form of pest control.

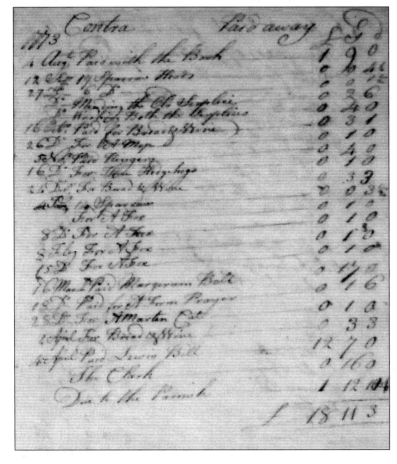

Fig. 5 Extract from the Bathwick Churchwardens Accounts Book for 1766-1807, dated April 1773, showing payments for "14 sparrows heads ... a fox ... a marten cat". Sparrows, foxes, pine martens and other small creatures were considered vermin. As the 18th century 'Enclosure Acts' took effect and 'commoner rights' began to disappear, payments for trapping and killing these animals and birds became an important part of a poor family's income. (*Somerset Record Office, D/P/batw.m4/1/1*)

A general study of these old documents suggests that until about 1788 the parish was just about able to make ends meet but was not affluent. However, as new buildings were completed and the rich and titled moved in, Bathwick acquired a new and more fashionable image. Gradually old familiar names disappear from the pages of the accounts books and reappear in the burial records.

In the latter part of the 18th century Bathwick was still a country parish including the small 'street' village of about 250 inhabitants, 45 dwellings, a church and an inn. A mill stood on the bank of the River Avon near its western boundary. By early 1800 the old village had all but been lost to Georgian development and by 1838 there was no common land.[8]

In 1801, by an Act of Parliament (followed by several other Acts in the ensuing years), parish administration was gradually altered until the 1814 Act[9] in Bath came into force. By 1815 most of the duties of the vestry had become the responsibility of the

'Board of Commissioners and Watch Committee'. This body of men met monthly in the Police Office at George's Place on Bathwick Hill to regulate

> *Policing, Watering, Lighting, Cleansing and Watching the several Streets &c in the Parish of Bathwick, and for removing and preventing Nuisances, Annoyances ...*

By 1819 two night constables and eight night watchmen patrolled the streets of Bathwick, although this figure soon increased to 16 watchmen. Constables were paid £7 5s 3d per quarter whilst a night watchman received about £3 10s. Each man was equipped with a rattle, costing three shillings and sixpence, with which he could summon assistance if necessary. Basic parish fire fighting equipment such as street 'fire plugs' and a 'waterpond'[10] was also provided at this time.

WANTED, for the Parish of **BATHWICK**,

A Suitable Person to fill the united Offices of SURVEYOR, CONSTABLE, and COLLECTOR of Rates and Assessments under the Bathwick Police Act of Parliament. The salary will be £85 per year, with the use of a good House connected with the Police-Office, in which the Person when appointed must reside. The Police Hat and Coat must be worn: and security in the amount of £500 will be required.—Any Person desirous of serving the above offices, must attend at the Police-Office in the parish of Bathwick, on MONDAY the 6th day of December next, with proper testimonials of character and ability.

Further explanation will be given on application to Mr Page, clerk to the Commissioners, at his office, No. 9, Fountain-buildings, Bath. By order of the Commissioners,

Police Office, Bathwick, Nov. 1, 1819. J. PAGE, Clerk

Fig. 6 (*above*) *The Bath Chronicle,* November 1819. (*Bath Central Library*)

In addition to these changes, which brought to the parish many benefits that were already in place in the city, power and authority shifted from the vestry towards civil administration through National Parliamentary Reform until 1835 when a fully urbanized Bathwick finally lost its rural identity and became part of the City of Bath.

Fig. 7 (*right*) Election poster for the Parish Churchwarden, 1846. At this time Joseph Lansdown had been in office as churchwarden for two years but at a vestry meeting on 16th April 1846 his re-election was opposed and a Poll was demanded by Mr Withers, another nominee. Interestingly the Poll stated that "Ladies being Rate-payers are entitled and solicited to Vote", this being long before women were allowed the vote in parliamentary elections. (*Somerset Record Office, D/P/batw.m8/4/6*)

BATHWICK
CHURCH-RATE
CASE.

ELECTION
OF THE
Parish Churchwarden.

LADIES and GENTLEMEN,

Go to the Poll, at the Police Office, Sydney Wharf, EARLY To-Morrow (FRIDAY), and SATURDAY, and

VOTE FOR WITHERS,

Who has offered to meet the Trustees in a proper friendly spirit, and settle the matter *amicably*, and thereby save the Parish immense costs.

VOTE for WITHERS

Who has pledged himself to the Vestry Meeting this Morning to take care of the Interests of the Parish in every way, and save it £250 per Annum.

Pay your Rates and go to the Poll, and do not be cajoled by LANSDOWN, CHILCOT, MILSOM, and Co., who wish to embroil the Parish in every way, but do your duty as Ratepayers, and the Victory will be gained, the Church-Rate Case settled, and thousands saved.

BATHWICK; Thursday Evening, April 16.

JOHN AND JAMES KEENE, PRINTERS, KINGSMEAD STREET, BATH.

THE PULTENEY PURCHASE

In 1553 the Manor of Bathwick in the County of Somerset was acquired by the Neville family, passing in 1691 to the Earl of Essex[11] and thence by purchase to the Hon. William Pulteney MP, later Earl of Bath, in 1727. The sum paid by Pulteney was £12,000, which included the Manors of Wrington, Burrington and Ubley and the hamlet of Wolley (*sic*). At the time of purchase Bathwick was recorded as containing 600 acres of land let at a yearly rent of £241, also a mill on the River Avon let at £12 and a piece of land at Walcot. Farming included the rearing of sheep and woodland coppicing, and large plots of the land were tended by city traders as market gardens.

Fig. 8 Hon. William Pulteney Esq. (1684-1764). (*Private collection, Bath*)

Before the introduction of topographical maps, most parish boundaries were marked by positioning boundary stones and perambulation by 'Beating of the Bounds' – a ceremony which was carried on annually by vestry officers and parishioners. Pulteney had the Manor lands surveyed and the earliest known detailed map of Bathwick drawn for him.[12] Throughout the following years he set about making changes to the lengthy leaseholds and tenures held within the parish and introduced shorter ones. Although William Pulteney is known to have visited Bath during his ownership there is no evidence to suggest that either he or any subsequent Lords of the Manor of Bathwick ever resided in the parish.

In 1742 Bathwick contained 20 houses and villagers paid a yearly rent plus "Herriotts (*sic*) of Best beast(s)" according to acreage of land occupied.[13] There was also "Common of pasture land" for grazing sheep. At this time the only access by road to and from Bathwick and the city was via the turnpike road that ran from 'Clardon' [Claverton] through the parish of Lyncombe and Widcombe and over the St. Laurence Bridge (Old Bridge). Under the terms of an Act passed in c.1740 tolls were payable on this and all other turnpike roads and the revenue used to repair them. A scale of charges for traffic allowed broad-wheeled vehicles to pay less than those with narrow wheels and certain exemptions included

> *all Waggons and other Carriages Horses and other Cattle laden with materials for mending the Roads, Corn in the Straw, or Manure (except Lime) and Implements of Husbandry ...*

Fig. 9 A section from *The South-east Prospect of the City of Bath* by Samuel and Nathaniel Buck, 1734. The old village of Bathwick is seen on the right; the mill on the river bank is at the far left, just below the weir. The people are picnicking in fields at Claverton Down. Note the difference in the two parties. The group on the right are visibly more affluent than those on the left where the boy has a line of small birds, possibly sparrows to be presented for payment from parish accounts. (*Bath Record Office*)

The inhabitants of Bathwick used the Claverton turnpike road to carry all their produce to the Bath markets and bring back the "Dung and Soil" (used as manure). They reached the turnpike by means of a lane known as

> *Bathwicke Lane, extending near half a mile from the said village to the end of the said Lane, where it joins the Turnpike road and from thence to the said City upon the Turnpike road is only about two furlongs ...*

but which for most of the year was "ruinous and Founderous" and so narrow in places that it was only possible for narrow-wheeled vehicles to pass with difficulty and not at all negotiable for broad wheels. This meant that not only were the villagers of Bathwick obliged to pay the higher tolls but also were excluded from claiming any exemptions when they actually made use of the turnpike road for barely two furlongs (a quarter of a mile). In 1757 they petitioned Parliament for powers either to have the lane widened and repaired or to be allowed to claim the lower toll charges and exemptions.[14]

> TO be LETT, at Lady-Day next, the very plea-
> santly situated FIELDS, known by the name of TERRY
> FARM, with never-falling springs of soft water, rising on the
> upper side, commanding a very pleasing prospect of Bath and its
> environs; situated near the turnpike bar, Bathwick-lane, eligible
> either for building or pleasure gardens.
>   For further particulars, enquire of John Lockyer, carver and
> gilder, John-street, Bath.   [766

Fig. 10 *The Bath Chronicle*, June 1788. (*Bath Central Library*)

Sir William's Plan

William Pulteney, Earl of Bath, died in 1764, and his estate passed first to his brother, General Harry Pulteney. In 1767 the General died without issue and Frances Pulteney, daughter of his cousin Daniel, succeeded to the ownership. Frances had, in 1760, married William Johnstone who, on his wife's inheritance, took the Pulteney name.[15]

The estate was still outwardly almost unchanged from the 1727 purchase for, until the time of his death, the only development William Pulteney had allowed in Bathwick was the Spring Gardens Pleasure Resort c.1750, laid out on the West Mead, now the Recreation Ground.[16]

William Johnstone Pulteney was a man of great vision who planned to open up the parish and build a 'new town' by leasing land to investors and builders. His scheme depended on good access to the city via a new bridge across the river. Achieving this required negotiations with Bath Corporation about supplying water from springs on Bathwick Down and the provision of a new city gaol.[17]

Fig. 11 Pulteney Bridge (built 1769-1774), pictured c.1955. (*BLHS Archives*)

By 1774 both bridge and prison were more or less complete but with the unstable economic climate of that time almost none of the hoped-for investment was forthcoming. The development then lay dormant for the next ten years, leaving the prison to stand splendid but alone in the Bathwick meadows and the new bridge no more than a direct route to the pleasure grounds of Spring Gardens and Bathwick Villa. Little else appears to have changed in the parish and the village remained a quiet place for a few more years. Merchants and traders, however, needed to get produce to the city markets and although it was now easier to cross the river via the new bridge, it was nonetheless risky. On the Bathwick side the access ramp was

Fig. 12 (*left above*) An old spring marker in Bathwick Wood, pictured in 2003. (*BLHS Archives*)

Fig. 13 (*right*) The spring head in Bathwick Wood, 2003. (*BLHS Archives*)

Fig. 14 Section from *A Map of the Manor of Bathwick in the County of Somerset, drawn for William Pulteney Esq.* (c.1770). This section shows Spring Gardens at no.91 and the mill at no.92. The boatstall is across the River Avon but the new bridge is not yet in place. (*Bath Record Office*)

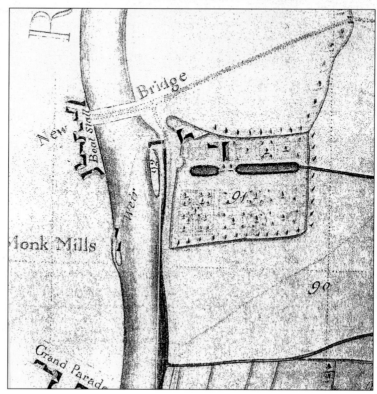

unfenced and dangerous and the mud-rutted roadway, though fairly negotiable in summer, became almost impassable during winter and remained so for many years. There was no further construction work until 1784, two years after Henrietta Laura Pulteney, daughter of William Johnstone and Frances Pulteney, inherited the estate from her mother.

At first investors were cautious and from then until 1787 only eight building leases were granted. A year later, however, this number had increased to 32,[18] mostly for houses in Great Pulteney Street and Henrietta Street.

Of the early leases issued, one was to George Clark and William Phillips to

> *dig stone in a quarry ... on the upper part of Smallcomb Wood for building on six plots in Boatstall Meadows lying east side of the River Avon and other sundry houses in Bathwick ...*

and on the same day William Mathews was also granted lease to quarry stone from Smallcombe Wood

> *in a quarry there situate and marked out by posts and Boundary stones there set up and affixed by the surveyor* [Thomas Baldwin] *of the said Henrietta Laura Pulteney ... and to build in Boatstall Meadows eleven substantial mesuages with offices and vaults ...*[19]

Boatstall Meadows, then part of Bathwick Mead, took its name from the boatstall which originally occupied the stretch of river bank near where the Podium building stands today.

Fig. 15 In the 18th century this was the site of an ancient access to the boatstall.
(*Terry Hardick, 2007*)

Since the land being developed was low-lying natural flood plain, the river was banked and road levels raised on arched vaults, for which purpose millions of bricks were used.[20] This elevation is particularly noticeable in Johnstone Street and around Argyle Street, Laura Place and Great Pulteney Street where there are both basements and sub-basements.

In 1788 the foundation stone for Laura Place was laid by Henrietta Laura Pulteney and during the event church bells rang and guns in Spring Gardens were fired

> *amidst the acclamation of the populace, who were treated with plenty of strong beer delivered from the foundation stone in pails. A very elegant entertainment afterwards was given by Mr Pulteney to the Builders and their friends at the Bear Inn.*
> (*The Bath Chronicle, 3rd April 1788*)

16

Fig. 16 (*above*) A section from *View of Bath* by Samuel I. Grimm (1788). This view shows Georgian development in progress. Note the arches to the right of the completed new bridge revealing how the road levels had to be raised. (*©The British Library Board. All rights reserved 01/02/2008. Add 15546, f90*)

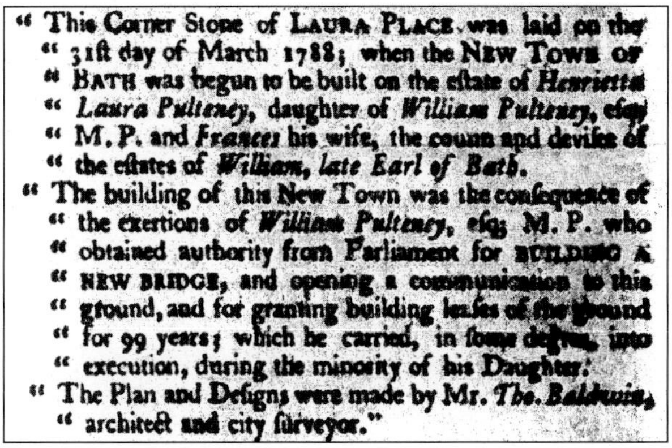

" This Corner Stone of LAURA PLACE was laid on the
" 31ft day of March 1788; when the NEW TOWN OF
" BATH was begun to be built on the eftate of Henrietta
" Laura Pulteney, daughter of William Pulteney, efq;
" M. P. and Frances his wife, the coufin and devifee of
" the eftates of William, late Earl of Bath.
" The building of this New Town was the confequence of
" the exertions of William Pulteney, efq; M. P. who
" obtained authority from Parliament for BUILDING A
" NEW BRIDGE, and opening a communication to this
" ground, and for granting building leafes of the ground
" for 99 years; which he carried, in fome degree, into
" execution, during the minority of his Daughter.
" The Plan and Defigns were made by Mr. Tho. Baldwin,
" architect and city furveyor."

Fig. 17 (*left*) 'Corner Stone of Laura Place'. (*The Bath Chronicle, 3rd April 1788*)

Bathwick Quarries

For centuries stone has been extracted from the Downs surrounding the city of Bath and early quarrying within this parish took place wherever deposits were readily available. Before Sir William's scheme, hauling the stone and gravel needed for small jobs around the village was usually done by one man and a boy with horse and cart, though sometimes a whole family would help out. There were gravel pits near the river in Villa Fields. Stone from Bathwick Down and Smallcombe Vale was mostly inferior oolite used for walling and roads. Although some greater oolite suitable for house building was quarried from woods in the upper region of Smallcombe Vale, most of the Bath stone used in the construction of 18th and 19th-century Bathwick is thought to have come from Ralph Allen's quarries at Combe Down. Today the remains of some of the Bathwick quarries can still be seen at the top of North Road, although large 20th-century houses now occupy most of the site.

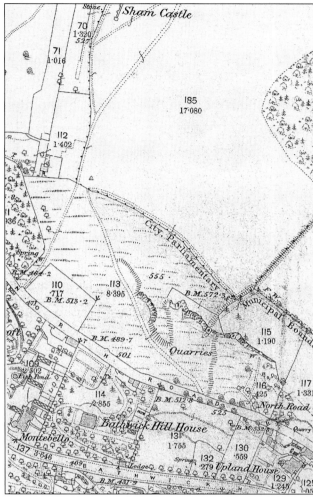

Fig. 18 (*left*) A section from the 1886 OS map showing some of the Bathwick quarries. These surface quarries were quite extensive. In 1855 an agreement was drawn up between Lord Powlett (Duke of Cleveland) and Ralph Shuttleworth Allen, of Bathampton, to allow carts to cross Bathwick land by track-way to reach the quarries on Bathampton Down. (*Bath Record Office*)

Fig. 19 (*below left*) The track-way still exists and is now part of a public footpath leading to Sham Castle. The castle, built for Ralph Allen in 1762, stands on land bordering the Sham Down. (*BLHS Archives*)

Fig. 20 (*below right*) Stone pillar remains of the Bathwick quarries adjacent to the bridleway on the corner of Quarry Road and North Road in 2007. Quarry Road is part of the University of Bath complex and was blasted out during its development in 1963. (*BLHS Archives*)

Fig. 21 An aerial photograph taken on 10th August 1945. The boundaries of Bathwick, Bathampton and Claverton meet just beyond the open area next to the clump of trees (mid far right) – see Fig.18 opposite. (*English Heritage, NMR – RAF Photography*)

The Georgians and later the Victorians gathered huge quantities of water-worn stone from Bathampton Down to form rockeries and other park and garden features, including a grotto that once stood in Sydney Gardens.

By the end of the 18th century hundreds of journeymen quarrymen and masons were attracted to the parish in search of work and many settled here. In 1790 William Hulance dug stone from his quarry at Combe Down[21] to build houses in Bathwick Street and in 1793 John Pinch, then a joiner by trade[22], arrived in Bath from Cornwall to work under the direction of the architect Thomas Baldwin.

Fig. 22 A mason's mark in the Kennet & Avon Canal tunnel under Sydney Road. (*BLHS Archives*)

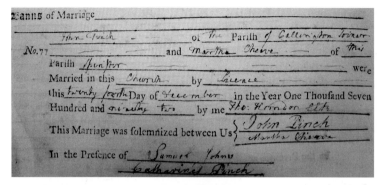

Fig. 24 *View of Bath from Bathwick Hill*, watercolour (c.1825) attributed to Charles Marshall (1806-1890). On the right, note the cut stone from the Bathwick quarries waiting to be loaded onto horse-drawn carts and transported to the building site. (*Private collection, Bath*)

Local Difficulties

Through the years the Pulteney development suffered regular setbacks, sometimes severe and prolonged. The huge cost of raising the roads above flood level and problems with bad weather frequently made work impossible and progress slow, incurring a liability for penalties often waived by Miss Pulteney.

Initially our Vestry minutes record little of the Pulteney project or its progress. The parishioners generally appeared to be more concerned with the worsening state of their ancient parish church which was urgently in need of repair. Later on there is, perhaps, a hint of anger and frustration about the general state of the parish and the way in which the 'Poore House' in Grove Street was demolished, apparently leaving the inhabitants to fend for themselves. Two entries in the churchwardens' accounts book for 30th May and 29th July 1790 record the event and although there are no other references to the incident, a later Vestry minute resolves *that Poor People as have Pay from the Parish, be supplied with such clothing as may be necessary, and John Warren and his wife belonging to this Parish, being aged and past their labour may have four shillings per week for their support and that also Firing be provided for the use of the Poor in general, As shall be judged Proper by the Overseers.*

Problems continued to affect the development and in 1793 the Bath bank crash brought financial chaos and widespread bankruptcy. Construction was abandoned almost overnight leaving large sections of the parish as neglected building sites and half-built roads that went nowhere!

Fig. 25 (*right*) An extract from the Bathwick Churchwardens Accounts Book 1766-1807. This entry, dated 30 May 1790, repeats the words of a report of the previous day's meeting. The comments suggest a hint of frustration at the re-development (and destruction) taking place within the parish at that time. (*Somerset Record Office, D/P/batw.m4/1/1*)

Fig. 26 *Bath, Grove Street &c*, print by John Hill (c.1804, after J.C Nattes).
(*©Victoria Art Gallery, Bath & North East Somerset Council*)

The effects of this disaster were dreadful. With no work, men were unable to support their families and hundreds went hungry. The parish, already struggling to care for its own poor, became almost overwhelmed and neighbouring parishes also suffered.

Although by 1795 there was partial recovery and construction resumed, economic instability because of the ongoing wars with France and the problem of providing parish relief for the poor and unemployed went unresolved. In 1797, in an effort to ease this burden, Bathwick moved to join with the parishes of Lyncombe and Widcombe and of St. James to accommodate the ever increasing numbers of "wandering vagrants" and a "house of industry" was suggested

> for persons who are not objects of parochial aid and who are able to support
> themselves in a life of industry ...[23]

Little information survives of this plan which was never fully implemented, and it was not until 1837 that the Union Workhouse at Midford Road was built.[24]

Complaints about the condition of the roads and the lack of them also continued and the Vestry decided to apply directly to Sir William Pulteney for

> his consent in Making a Roadway from Bathwick field into Henrietta Street for
> general accommodation and that an estimate of the expense thence to be taken by
> Mr Pinch ...

By 1799 the dire condition was reported of

> a certain piece of road leading from Mr Falkners Mills in this parish and by whom
> the road might be repaired ... a report from the Constable of the Hundreds of this
> Parish and signed by the Rector and Churchwardens should be sent to Mr Pinch
> for the information of Mr Pulteney that the road should be repaired by him and
> not the Parish.[25]

In 1800, after a long spell of bad weather and flooding, one of the supporting piers on the north side of the bridge collapsed and the whole side had to be rebuilt.

Work on the bridge took nearly two years to complete, and although surviving papers and letters belonging to Sir William point to efforts on his part to address the situation, by July 1802 the Bathwick parish clerk had received a curt letter from the Deputy Clerk of the Peace for the County stating that

> this part of Pulteney bridge which lies
> within this Parish is a Nuisance and ...
> unless the same is repaired the inhabitants
> will be Indicted at the next general quarter
> sessions of the said County ...[26]

It was agreed to adopt immediately

> such measures as may at the said Vestry
> meeting be thought expedient for the
> protection of the Parishioners ...

Fig. 27 From *The Bath Chronicle Weekly*, November 1800. (*Bath Central Library*)

and also resolved

> *First that there is no necessity for this Parish to communicate the contents of the Clerk of the Peace's letter to Sir Wm Pulteney Bt before it is acted upon by the Parish ...*

In September payments made to a local contractor "George Head for work done" and "Mrs Bolwells bill for Beer for the Workmen – £2 11s 3d"[27] indicate that repairs were done at the expense of the parish and the threat of prosecution removed.[28]

Laying Out the 'New Town'

Many of the Bathwick streets we know today have names connected with the Pulteney family. Those with the prefix 'Sydney' are named after Thomas Townsend, Viscount Sydney, British Home Secretary (1783-84[29]), a political associate of the Pulteneys.

By 1792 the New Town had begun to take shape and a few property advertisements confidently proclaimed newly-built houses for sale as standing in 'Newtown'.

Construction then commenced on the first rank of a series of eight terraces intended to surround Sydney House (later Sydney Hotel) and Sydney Gardens, both built c.1795.

The first terrace of Sydney Place, designed by Thomas Baldwin, was finally completed in 1795 and initially comprised 14 houses. Later conversions have subsequently reduced the number to 12!

Fig. 28 *View from Sydney Place* (north side, c.1890). From 1801 to 1804 No.4 Sydney Place was the home of Jane Austen. Look closely at the terrace today and the later alterations are just visible. (*©Bath in Time – Bath Central Library collection*)

The second terrace, formerly known as New Sydney Place, was built in 1808 and is the last phase of a plan which was never finished. Leases here were the first to be granted by William Henry (Harry) Vane, Earl of Darlington. The architect was John Pinch and on completion the main contractor, James Goodridge, became the first tenant of the westernmost house. The 11 houses in this rank are numbered 93-103 and though there are no later conversions to be seen, there were once 12 as No.104 stands across the road on the corner of Great Pulteney Street where re-numbering in 1909 made it part of the street on which it was erected. Although the other terraces were never built, 'Sydney Place' can still be seen carved on it and on the house which occupies the opposite corner of Great Pulteney Street – both waiting patiently!

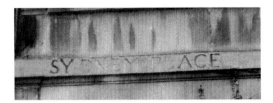

Figs. 29 & 30 (*above*) 'Sydney Place' cut into the stonework of Nos.41 and 41a Great Pulteney Street. (*Terry Hardick 2007*)

Fig. 31 (*right*) From *The Bath Chronicle*, 7th December 1820. The description of the various floors of the house includes the attic storey with closets, down to the ground floor and garden and an enclosed stable yard, stall stabling for eight horses, a double coach-house and harness rooms plus accommodation for five man-servants. (*Bath Central Library*)

Noble FREEHOLD MANSION, SYDNEY PLACE,
In the City of BATH, with immediate possession.
To be SOLD by AUCTION, by Mr. WILLOCK
At the White Lion Inn in the city of Bath, on Thursday the 14th of December, at 12 o'clock,

THE Spacious Elegant FREEHOLD HOUSE, most eligibly situate the Upper End on SYDNEY PLACE, in the City of Bath, the residence of

Her late Majesty QUEEN CHARLOTTE

Containing six neatly-papered chambers, with closets, and a lobby, on the attic story; four airy, cheerful, neatly-finished bedchambers, a dressing-room and closets on the two pair floor; two noble lofty drawing-rooms, a boudoir, ante-room, and conservatory, on the principal floor; an entrance-hall, large well-proportioned eating-rooms, saloon, and spacious library, with a bath-room and closets, on the ground floor; a handsome stone staircase, and a profusion of domestic offices, for the complete accommodation of a family of the first distinction; with very excellent cellaring; a large garden, and an enclosed stable yard, stall stabling for eight horses, double coach-house, harness-rooms, with five men servants' chambers and lofts over them.——To be viewed till the sale, and particulars may be had on the premises of Messrs Bayly and Savage solicitors, of Mr. Pinch, architect, in Bath, and at the place of sale; at the office of William Leake, esq: Devonshire-street, Portland-place, and of Mr. Willock, No. 25, Golden square, London. [1811

Daniel Street is named after Daniel Pulteney (1685-1731), grandfather of Henrietta Laura Pulteney. He was a Member of Parliament and was once reputed to have been a spy for Queen Anne. This street was originally part of the plan for Frances Square and Frances Street and the first three houses were designed by Thomas Baldwin before the 1793 bank crisis when this scheme was abandoned. Frances Street later became Sutton Street, thus leaving Frances Pulteney (Henrietta Laura's mother) without a Bathwick street or building dedicated to her.

The first lease for Daniel Street, granted on 26th March 1792[30], was for the end house which soon after completion became the *Pulteney's Arms* with a coach-house and stable at its rear. John Bagshaw, the first landlord of the inn, remained there until his death in 1809, when he became the first person to be buried in the newly-opened additional burial ground in Henrietta Road, now known as Old St. Mary's Churchyard.

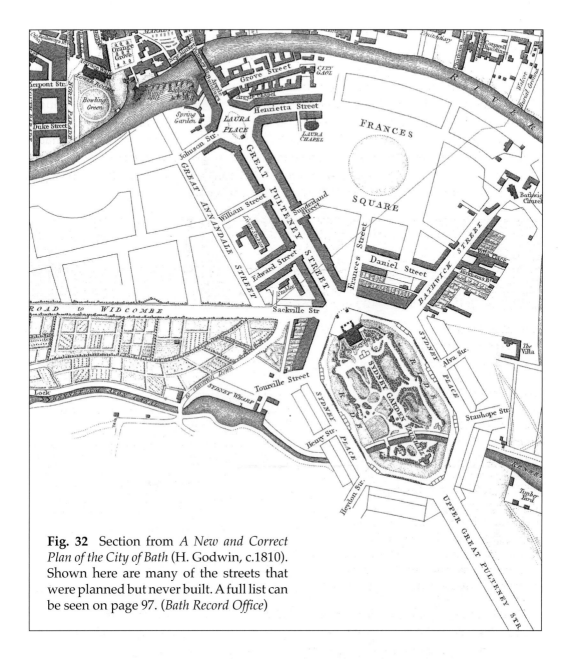

Fig. 32 Section from *A New and Correct Plan of the City of Bath* (H. Godwin, c.1810). Shown here are many of the streets that were planned but never built. A full list can be seen on page 97. (*Bath Record Office*)

The two adjoining houses were also built before the bank crash halted construction. In 1810 work resumed on the remainder of the street to the design of John Pinch and by 1820 the street was more or less complete.

In later years during the German air raids on Bath in April 1942, a high explosive bomb fell at the junction of Daniel Street and Sutton Street. The landlord of *The Pulteney Arms*, Mr Longstrat, was injured and houses at the southern end suffered extensive damage. Other buildings in the vicinity, including houses in Great Pulteney Street, were also affected and had windows and doors blown out by the blast. Henrietta Park was also hit but fortunately no fatalities resulted.

Fig. 33 (*right*) The rear view of Daniel Street and **Fig. 34** (*below*) the rear of Bathwick Street, c.1930. Most of these protrusions were extra 'loos'. By the late 18th century most Georgian town houses were being constructed with a good clean water supply and a 'bath'. Water closets also became very popular and eventually every house had to have one! The Georgian architect John Eveleigh was one of the first to advertise them in houses that he designed. (*Bath Record Office*)

Fig. 35 Daniel Street, c.1900. Throughout the 19th century many of these houses were used as lodging houses. By 1858 this street had the dubious distinction of having a pub at each end! (*The Bath Chronicle*)

Fig. 36 (*right*) The corner of Daniel Street and Bathwick Street in 2007. In the mid 19th century a beer-house known as *The Rifleman's Arms* occupied this corner. (*BLHS Archives*)

Planning for an Invasion

In 1803 the threat loomed of an imminent invasion by the French. This brought into effect the 'Defence of the Country Act' requiring all towns and villages to put contingency plans in place, and the Bathwick Vestry committee duly met to consider how

> to determine on the best measures for enabling the Ministry, Churchwardens and Overseers of the Poor to assist the Constables, Tythingmen and Peace Officers of this Parish in the making out Returns to a certain Precept and Schedule delivered to them by order of the Lieutenant of the County of Somerset requiring under certain heads Various Matters and things to be done for the general defence of the County in the case of actual invasion of the Enemy.
>
> Resolved that the constable and those above mentioned make the required Returns by desiring each Male Resident in each family by personal application at their Houses to engage 'wanting' to perform some of the following duties –
>
> 1 Persons residing within 15 miles of the County engage to drive all livestock of the County to proper places of delegation and to destroy or remove all other means of the enemy's Subsistence.
>
> 2 To bear Arms and to Assemble when the enemy has landed to act in concert with His Majesty's forces.
>
> 3 To serve as Yeomen; to be provided with pickaxes spades billhooks etc.
>
> 4 To form part of a Corps of Guides on horseback being well acquainted with the country parts, lands etc.
>
> 5 Engage to supply such a number of Waggons, Carts, Horses etc.
>
> 6 Engage as a Miller to furnish such a quantity of ready made flour as he has on hand over and above the immediate want of customers.
>
> 7 Engage (as a Baker) to bake and deliver such quantity of bread or the like condition.
>
> 8 Engage as a barge or boat Master to aid the public service in law of Invasion by supplying such boats, barges for the conveyances of troops or horses.

Resolved that such of the inhabitants who are disposed to form a Company of Riflemen to serve the Parish of Bathwick will sign their names in a book now produced for that purpose and that an application be made to the Government for a man to drill the Company ...[31]

A Volunteer Corps was formed and drilled regularly in Villa Fields under the direction of the Colonel Commandant, John Glover of Pulteney Street. Despite an increase in population, the parish was unable to raise the number required and for being just three men short had to pay £60,

the penalty incurred by the Parish thro the deficiency in raising the proper quota of men for the Army Reserve and Militia ...

Fortunately the feared invasion did not happen. After the defeat of Napoleon in 1815 most volunteer units were disbanded, although the Bath Volunteer Regiment, which included Bathwick, continued as the Bath Volunteer Rifle Corps until 1826.[32] Later the Corps became known as the First and Second Bath & Bathwick Somerset Rifle Corps.

From Pulteney to Vane

In 1808 Henrietta Laura Pulteney, Countess of Bath, died without issue, Bathwick, with other extensive estates, passing to her kinsman and heir, Lord William Henry (Harry) Vane 1766-1842, 3rd Earl of Darlington and (later) Duke of Cleveland.[33]

The line of succession from Pulteney to Vane is a complex one traced back to Anne (1663-1745), aunt of William Pulteney (Earl of Bath), who married Charles (1662-1730), 1st Duke of Cleveland. In turn their daughter Grace Fitzroy married Henry Vane, 3rd Baron Barnard (of Raby Castle) and 1st Earl of Darlington. On the death of General Pulteney in 1767 the (3rd) Earl then became the male descendant to the Pulteney line and following this he and his descendants were named heirs on expiry of the female Pulteney line which subsequently occurred with the death of Henrietta Laura.[34]

Fig. 37 Lord William Harry Vane (1766-1842), 3rd Earl of Darlington, 1st Duke of Cleveland. (*Published by kind permission of The Lord Barnard, TD*)

The Vane succession marked the beginning of a new era. For over 80 years, since William Pulteney's purchase, Bathwick had been in the ownership of the Pulteney family, but from here on architectural styles and street names reflect the change.[35]

By 1810 development had reached Bathwick Hill, then still a rough and lonely road with a rivulet running down one side, known only as 'the road to Claverton'.

The ground has been marked out for making a road 60 feet wide from the end of Pulteney-street to Claverton-down and that by an ascent almost imperceptible through Lord Darlington's estate. We are happy to add, that this beautiful down will soon be again accessible to the inhabitants of Bath ...[36]

This was now the age of transport and the opening of the Kennet & Avon Canal[37], followed later by the construction of the Bristol to Paddington railway line through Bathwick, had a huge effect on the parish.

In 1834 as plans for the Great Western Railway were drawn up, an Act of Parliament for the acquisition of land for its construction was obtained. At Bathwick this included tunnelling under Bathwick Hill at Bathwick Terrace and Raby Place. The Duke of Cleveland was bitterly opposed to the route of the railway over his land and argued furiously against it but to no avail, and construction went ahead.

Fig. 38 A Kennet & Avon Canal Company boundary stone still in position near the canal bank. (*BLHS Archives*)

Bathwick New Church

The foundation stone of the new parish church was laid in September 1814 though because of the later building of the chancel in 1875 this is no longer visible. A brass inscription plate soldered onto the stone contains a list of 23 names including those of Lord Darlington; Reverend Peter Gunning; John Pinch, architect; Walter Harris, builder; and various other benefactors and members of the Vestry. As the stone was lowered into position coins, medals and tokens were placed beneath it.

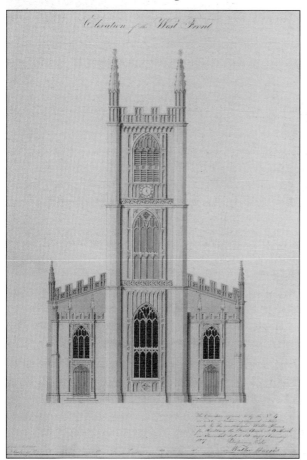

Fig. 39 (*left*) 'Bathwick New Church' from plans by John Pinch dated 1817. (*Somerset Record Office, D/P/batw.m8/2/1*)

Fig. 40 (*below*) An extract from the Bathwick Churchwardens Accounts Book of 1811. This entry, made on 2nd December 1811, shows payment for John Pinch's original plans which were subsequently modified. (*Somerset Record Office, D/P/batw.m4/1/2*)

The inscription reads:

GLORY TO GOD IN THE HIGHEST – ON EARTH PEACE.
The most sanguinary conflict ever recorded in the annals of History has ceased,
and the downfall of Napoleon, the Despot of France, had taken place, when the
Nations of Europe became united in the bond of Peace. At such as a joyful period,
and on the 1st day of September, in the year of our Lord 1814, the foundation-
stone of Bathwick New Church, dedicated to Saint Paul, was laid.[38]

In 1815, following the laying of the stone, an Act of Parliament for building a new church and workhouse was obtained[39] (with an amendment added on 23rd May 1817) but here disagreements brought construction to an abrupt standstill. Many thought the building was too costly and also considered the dedication to Saint Paul "an act of vandalism" since "for nigh on nine hundred years the Parish had been under the patronage of St. Mary ..." and five years went by before the church was able to open its doors to a congregation. During this time the vestry clerk, Sam Evill, reasoned that as Lord Darlington had given land at the back of (New) Sydney Place for the building of a new and bigger church, it was far better to spend £10,000 on this than £3,000 restoring and enlarging the old church on the other side of the parish.

Construction finally resumed early in 1817 and William Harris, a local mason and builder, was contracted to complete the work to Pinch's plan at a cost of £8,000, exclusive of the foundations. At the same time the artist Benjamin Barker expressed his intention to produce the altarpiece. By 1818 the problem of the dedication was also solved when the demolition of the old church made it possible for the new parish church to be re-dedicated to St. Mary.

The official opening of the church, said to "comfortably accommodate fourteen hundred persons" was arranged for 4th February 1820 and attracted so much interest that admittance to the ceremony had to be regulated by ticket "for each of which not less than five shillings can be accepted ...". There were concerns that the building might be "damp and unfit", a constant problem in the old church. To eliminate this risk, fires complete with the installation of "a new principle by flues, which render the air of a comfortable and warm temperature" were kept burning for several months beforehand. The date turned out to be unpopular for two reasons. It was a Friday, widely accepted as 'an evil day', and also coincided with the Proclamation of Accession of George IV, scheduled to take place in the city at the same time and which many people wished to attend. However, both events went ahead as planned, although, much to the annoyance of the long-suffering and sober Bathwick parishioners, the Rector's solemn prayer was promptly followed by the firing of 21 rounds of cannon from the other party across the river!

At last Bathwick had a fine new parish church but the next problem was how to pay for it. Under the Acts of 1815 and 1817, powers were obtained to raise money for erecting the building on security of the Church Rate at the time and this fund was to be subsidised by a limited number of pew rents, leased at £100 and £50 respectively, which the church trustees could redeem over time. As there was no compulsion on the part of the owners to sell their pew leases back to the church, many found it convenient to hold on to them or include them in the sale of their houses and this put the parishioners in the unhappy situation of either being partially excluded from the church which they had helped build, or paying to sit in it!

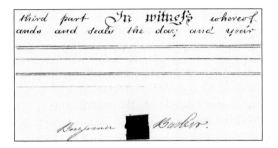

Freehold Dwelling HOUSE, (with immediate possession,)
in PULTENEY STREET, BATH;
A PEW in the NEW CHURCH, BATHWICK;
And SHARES in SYDNEY HOTEL and GARDEN
TO BE SOLD BY AUCTION,
By CHAS. PRITCHARD,
(Subject to such conditions as will be then and there produced,) by
order of the Executors of Mr. JAMES PETRIE deceased, on the
Premises, on Thursday July 23d, 1818, at 2 o'clock in the afternoon.

A Most Substantial and well-built FREEHOLD
DWELLING-HOUSE, situate and being
No. 71, in PULTENEY-STREET,

With Coach-house and 4-stall Stable, subject to a ground-rent of
£8 : 10s. : 6d. The House is in most excellent repair, and has the
advantage of an additional room on each floor; and contains

On the Basement, a kitchen, fitted with a range, smoke-jack,
oven, hot-plate, boiler, dresser, and shelves, and a range of
store closets on the outside; housekeeper's-room, with three
closets and numerous shelves; butler's-pantry, scullery, larder,
coal-house, laundry, wash-house with a boiler, beer and wine
cellars, and two spacious arched vaults ; the whole well supplied with fine spring water.

On the Ground-Floor, a dining-room, 17 feet 10 long, exclusive of a recess for a sideboard, and two large closets, 15
feet 8 wide, and 11 feet 8 high ; breakfast room adjoining, 17
feet 6 by 13 feet 10; and dressing-room, 12 feet 3 by 9 feet 9 ;
water-closet, with a plentiful supply of water.—A handsome
strong staircase leading to the drawing-rooms; the front room
21 feet 5 long, exclusive of two recesses, 17 feet 10 wide, and
12 feet high ; the back room, 18 feet 3 by 14 feet ; small ditto,
12 feet 9 by 12 feet 4.—A continuation of the stone staircase to
the chambers, the best front room is 18 feet 2 by 13 feet 8; the
small front, 13 feet 7 by 7 feet 5; back room, 18 feet 4 by 14
feet 1; and 10 feet 3 high.—Also, five servants' bedrooms.

A pleasant garden at the back of the house ; coach-house,
and four-stall stable, with a large loft, a coachman's room :
likewise a pump, with plenty of water.

A FREEHOLD PEW, to contain four Persons, in the New
CHURCH, BATHWICK.

TWO SHARES in SYDNEY GARDEN and HOTEL, (in
two lots); together with the proportionate part of the Fund,
amounting to about 2s. on each Share.—The Holder of each
Share has the right of admission to the Garden, and of intro-
ducing two friends, except Gala Days.

For particulars apply at the offices of Messrs. T. M. and J.
Cruttwell, solicitors; or to the auctioneer, 12, Westgate-street.

Fig. 41 (*above*) From 'Lease of Pew 41 South Gallery, St. Mary's Church, for 1 year ... May 1834, Benjamin Barker to Samuel Stoodley'. Benjamin Barker, artist, painted the *Nativity* which now hangs in the church's west gallery. This work was the new church's original altarpiece. (*By kind permission of the Rector and Churchwardens of St. Mary the Virgin Church, Bathwick*)

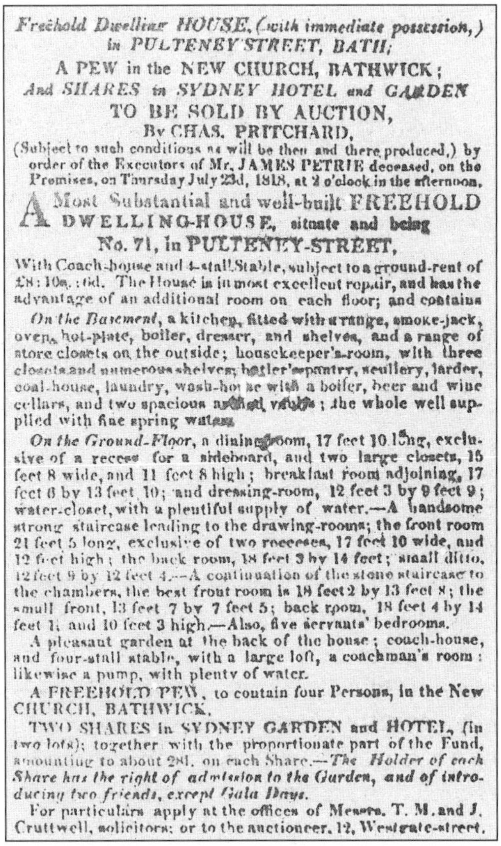

Fig. 42 (*right*) From *The Bath Chronicle*, July 1818. 'HOUSE TO BE SOLD ... A FREEHOLD PEW, to contain four Persons, in the New CHURCH, BATHWICK ...' (*Bath Central Library*)

The pew rent process turned out to be long and complicated. By 1864, of 1,000 sittings, only 300 were free. This situation remained almost unchanged until 1882, when the plight of non-renting members of the congregation who wished to sit in unoccupied pews was finally addressed. The result was summarized in the church magazine of that year:

> At the Easter Vestry a resolution was carried, with only one dissentient voice, that it
> would be desirable to throw the church open on Sundays as soon as the clergy and choir
> are in the chancel. By the present rule, which makes the church free at the beginning
> of the Psalms, much unnecessary interruption of the service takes place, and a large
> number of visitors and strangers are kept standing in the aisles and passages.

Clearly the original Acts had never intended such a state of affairs. Nevertheless it took decades to resolve and it was not until 1966 that pew rents finally ended.

Originally the body of the new church was arranged so that the congregation, backs to the altar, faced the pulpit and clerk's desk situated at the west end, a structure said to resemble "a huge candlestick with three sockets". For many years the clerk's desk was occupied by Henry White, a man, popular in the parish,

> of rotund form and jovial face and manner. With resonant voice he led the responses
> and "gave out the Psalms".[40]

In 1866 the box pews were replaced by the present lower ones which were then properly installed to face the altar at the east end and a new pulpit and reading desk. Ten years later the present chancel and altar were built.

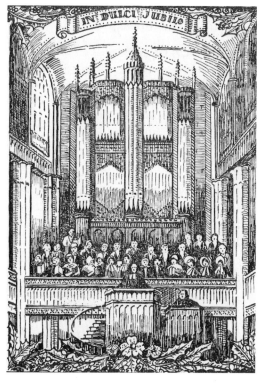

Fig. 43 MARY LAWRENCE
Died Feby 4th 1860.
aged 94.
For 68 years Pew Opener
at Bathwick,
in both the Old and New Churches.
To record the memory of Humble
Worth this stone is erected by the
Rector, Curates, Churchwardens
and some Parishioners.
St. Luke II 37v.
(*BLHS Archives*)

Fig. 44 An undated line drawing by Benjamin Maslen (1900-1983). This sketch shows how the pulpit and parish clerk's desk at the west end of the church, below the singers' gallery, might have looked prior to the mid-19th-century alterations. The free seating was situated behind the pulpit. (*By kind permission of the Rector and Churchwardens of St. Mary the Virgin Church, Bathwick*)

A Royal Visit

In the autumn of 1817 Queen Charlotte, consort of King George III, came to Bath to take the waters. The Queen, accompanied by their son, William, Duke of Clarence and daughter, Princess Elizabeth, had planned to stay in the Royal Crescent but as accommodation there was unavailable the next suitable choice was Bathwick where

> *Two houses in New Sydney Place (Lady Charlotte Denny's and Sir Gerrard Noel's) have been engaged for one month.*[41]

Despite continuing construction, including that of the new church, the parish was pleased to receive them. Streets were cleaned and an "unsightly" gravel pit opposite the "Queens house" in New Sydney Place was levelled and a tree and flagpole erected.

The flag, provided by "Batchellor, a tailor of Raby Place", cost the parish £12 9s. Captain Mainwaring reported:

> *two magnificent houses, at the extreme points of New Sydney Place were engaged*
> *for the accommodation of that illustrious personage and her suit. Several wagons,*
> *laden with superb furniture daily entered the city, for the purpose of decorating her*
> *Majesty's intended residences. A long list of fashionable arrivals were announced*
> *from day to day ...*[42]

On 21st October a troop of the 15th Light Dragoons entered the city followed by a second troop four days later. On 3rd November the royal party left Windsor for Bath:

> *They proceeded at a rapid rate. In the course of the afternoon a vast concourse left*
> *Bath to meet the Royal party, who entered the city at half-past four ...*

where the royal carriages, escorted by the Dragoons then drove through the city, across Pulteney Bridge and into Great Pulteney Street. En route they passed patriotically-decorated buildings and illuminations at the Guildhall and Laura Place. On reaching Sydney Place, a band played in front of Sydney House and

> *though the streets were crowded to excess, not the least riot or confusion appeared,*
> *nor were groups of well dressed females annoyed in their perambulations by the*
> *throwing of squibs, or the firing of guns ...*[43]

The visit was curtailed abruptly three days later with the news of the death during childbirth of Princess Charlotte Augusta, the Queen's granddaughter. The royal family immediately returned to Windsor and as they left Bath, muffled church bells tolled and shops were shuttered. When they returned a week later to complete their stay it was a more sombre affair though people were

> *drawn to Sydney Place in large numbers and could sometimes get a glimpse of the*
> *royal visitors as the windows were covered only by mere wisps of muslin.*

Fig. 46 (*above*) A medal struck for the visit of Queen Charlotte in 1817. (©*Bath in Time – Private collection, Bath*)

Fig. 45 (*left*) Queen Charlotte's Coat of Arms over the chemist's shop in Argyle Street (a protected pharmacy), pictured in 2007. The arms are made of Coade stone and were possibly commissioned for the royal visit to Bath in 1817. In the 1950s they were found in the basement of No.30 Milsom Street and given to Bath City Council where for years they were displayed at the foot of the main staircase of the Guildhall. During refurbishment of that building the arms were again put into storage. Eventually, however, through the efforts of the Bath Heraldic Society and the owner of the chemist's shop at that time, Mr Silk, they were cleaned and restored and placed in their present position in 1982. The arms are now in the care of the shop's owner, Mr B. Doshi. (*BHLS Archives*)

Bathwick Mews and Transport

The term 'mews' originally referred to the royal stables.[44] Likewise, in Georgian Bathwick, a mews – often known locally as 'stable lane' – was used to accommodate horses for transport. Here was stabling for up to eight or more horses at a time with living quarters for grooms and servants in the adjoining coach-houses, lofts and storerooms. Although the mews were busy during the hours of daylight, at night they were dark and shadowy and by the late Victorian period had become little more than run-down, hidden back streets.

At the beginning of the 19th century the general public could hire horse transport from at least 20 independent livery stables operating in Pulteney Mews, Henrietta Mews and Darlington Mews. Many of the early stable keepers came from Grove Street, where horse dealers, stables, coach makers and a veterinary surgeon were well established.

Fig. 47 Daniel Mews pictured in 2007. The newsagent's shop, once a coach-house and stables dating from 1810, was occupied in 1833 by John Jones 'Livery stable-keeper at the back of Old Sydney Place'. The building opposite was also once a coach-house and stables shared for many years by *The Barley Mow* (now called *The Barley*) and *The Crown Inn*. (*BLHS Archives*)

Figs. 48 & 49 Sydney Mews, c.1925. The coach-house here is the one described in Fig 31. The horses are standing in the adjoining stables. (*Norman Saunders collection*)

One of the first livery stable proprietors in Grove Street was Moses Pickwick, who started his well-known coaching and stable business there in 1790. By 1809 it had expanded into the city. Two other hard-working livery stable keepers in Grove Street, John Tasker and David White, also had extensive stables in Pulteney Mews. White often did other work in the parish such as supplying straw to the prison in Grove Street and the watchbox in Laura Place.[45]

By 1815 the two-horse Hackney coach, the earliest horse-drawn vehicle to be let for public hire, was licensed and widely used. Although this style of coach proved rather cumbersome for general use, it was almost 15 years before the 'fly' was invented.

The fly was a lightweight tin vehicle, designed to be faster and easier to manoeuvre than the heavier Hackney carriage. It was developed in about 1829 by William Ewens, an ironmonger and tinman of Westgate Street. Fitted onto wooden wheels, it was first drawn by two horses, though later modified for one. The first trial was carried out in Bathwick where it was driven down Great Pulteney Street and up Bathwick Hill, watched by a large crowd of bemused spectators.[46] Following this successful run the fly was used extensively for public transport for many years. The first official fly stand was set up in Laura Place. Later a second stand was established on the corner of Vane Street, facing St. Mary's Church, and a third at Cleveland Bridge.

Coachmen worked for long hours at a stretch, often in appalling conditions and traditionally had a reputation for being habitually drunk and reckless whilst driving.

In 1830 regulations for carrying the Bath public were tightened considerably and both owners and drivers were fined a minimum of ten shillings apiece if found to be in breach of any one of the rules. Good fly owners generally found it in their best interests to be compliant and by 1833 standards had improved enough for one local resident to observe:

> A Coachman drunk on his box is now a rarity – a coachman quite sober was, even within our memory, still more so.[47]

Drivers of public carriages wore a long blue frock coat and a black glazed hat with the number of the carriage painted on the front of the hat. When not hired, the horse and vehicle stood on the stand from eight in the morning until midnight.

Fig. 50 Great Pulteney Street and Laura Place, c.1890. Note the water cart refilling from the fountain in the foreground. Streets were watered at least daily to keep the dust down. A cab shelter (out of view on the right) was erected in 1884. (*BLHS Archives*)

In 1830 the average price of a horse for a fast coach was £23 (perhaps equivalent today to a car costing £17,750[48]) and an animal in good condition was said to be capable of covering 10 miles in 55 minutes. This resulted in gross overwork: the length of service barely reached four years and never exceeded it. Although it was possible to extend the working life to up to seven years if the horse were used with slower coaches or rested one day in four, this was not always done, and the life of the average working horse was short and harsh.

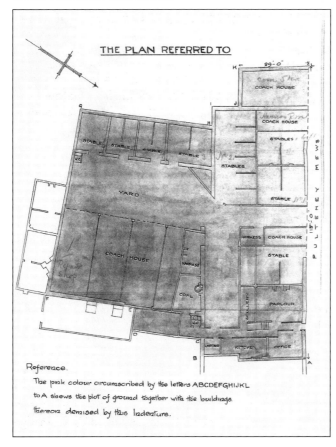

THE PLAN REFERRED TO

Reference.

The pink colour circumscribed by the letters ABCDEFGHIJKL to A shews the plot of ground together with the buildings thereon demised by this Indenture.

By the middle of the 19th century David White's stables in Pulteney Mews were taken over by John Strange and it is still just possible to pick out the words 'STRANGE'S STABLES' painted on the remaining part of the original building. In 1911 the Bath Carriage Works, a mix of horse and motor transport, occupied the premises, followed in 1920 by Mrs Bedford's Motor Car Works and in 1935 by A.E. Pollinger & Sons, Motor Engineers and Car Hire Service.

In 1972 most of the stable block was demolished and Gerrard's Buildings, a block of 18 apartments and garages, built on the site.[49] In Bathwick today the horses are all gone and most of the coach-houses are neat mews dwellings.

Fig. 51 (*above*) Pulteney Mews, plan from the Lease of coach-house and stable block occupied by Bath Carriage Company in 1911, formerly John Strange's Stables. Up to 25 horses could be stabled here at a time. (*Bath Record Office*)

Fig. 52 (*right*) From the *Bath Directory*, 1920. By this time many coach-houses and stables had been converted for use as garages or workshops and the age of horse transport was coming to an end.

Cleveland Bridge

In 1826, as the Georgian period drew to a close, it became clear that the 'New Town' would never be completed and so, perhaps fittingly, a bridge became the last notable achievement of that era in Bathwick. The idea was not new, for in 1784 Sir William Pulteney had seriously considered diverting traffic from the London Road to the city via Bathwick by bridge and imposing a toll. The Cleveland Bridge, designed by Henry Edmund Goodridge,[50] crosses the river on the estate's northern boundary, on land leased from the Earl of Darlington for 1,000 years.[51] Subscribers first agreed to raise the sum of £10,000 for "the purpose of erecting a private Bridge of Cast Iron with Stone Abutments ...".

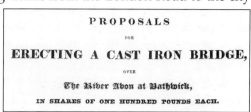

PROPOSALS

FOR

ERECTING A CAST IRON BRIDGE,

OVER

The River Avon at Bathwick,

IN SHARES OF ONE HUNDRED POUNDS EACH.

Fig. 53 (*above*) Heading from 'Bathwick Bridge, Deed of Settlement 24 May 1826'. (*Bath Record Office*)

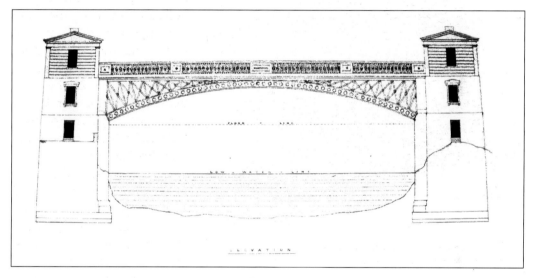

Fig. 54 Cleveland Bridge, drawing from the plans dated 1826. Opened in 1827, the bridge was first known as Bathwick Bridge. (*Bath Record Office*)

Clauses included the power to put tolls on the bridge, although Lord Darlington reserved the right to make it a free bridge within one year of completion if he so wished. Within two years of the agreement two lodges or toll houses with gates – one at each end of the bridge – were to be built[52] and no other building allowed within 50 feet of either of them. Lord Darlington also bound himself and his heirs

> *not to erect or suffer to be erected during the said term of 1000 years any Bridge across the river or allow any Passage or Ferry between Pulteney Bridge and the Parish of Bathampton, or in the Parishes of Bathampton or Walcot except the Bridge therein agreed to be built. Also to keep in repair, safe and proper and convenient roads and approaches to the bridge ... one of which roads lead to the turnpike road leading from Bath to London and the other to communicate with Bathwick Street and Henrietta Street.*

Cleveland Bridge remained in the ownership of the Bathwick Bridge Company until 1925 when it was purchased by the Bath Corporation in preparation for the removal of tolls. In 1928 work was carried out to strengthen the bridge for 20th-century traffic. A concrete bridge was constructed inside the iron structure thus making Cleveland Bridge 'a bridge within a bridge' and in 1929 the tolls were finally removed.

Fig. 55 (*above*) Testing Cleveland Bridge after completion of work to strengthen the bridge for 20th-century traffic. (*The Bath & Wilts Chronicle and Herald, 25th April 1929*)

Fig. 56 (*below*) '... freed from Tolls this afternoon'. (*The Bath & Wilts Chronicle and Herald, 20th June 1929*)

THE RISE OF VICTORIAN BATHWICK

The New Era

In the 1830s, as Regency architects took over the development of Bathwick, the unfinished streets built during the previous years were left as they stood. Instead, schools and roads were planned and large villas in the increasingly popular Italianate style appeared in the residential streets of Bathwick. Many of those houses can be seen today on Henrietta Road, Cleveland Walk and, most dramatically, on Bathwick Hill.

The opening of a new road from Warminster to Bath was announced in March 1833:

> *this will provide an easy and desirable approach to the centre of the City of Bath ...*
> *by which an easy access will be obtained through Claverton and Pulteney Street as*
> *the road through Hinton and Midford is both precipitous and in parts dangerous.*

Fig. 57 End of the Warminster and North Roads, c.1890. The large house was known as *North Road Lodge* and demolished sometime in the 1970s. (*BLHS Archives*)

This was followed by Pulteney Road, which was laid out shortly afterwards and trees planted. Barnard Villas was the first building in Pulteney Road and by 1836 the construction of the bridge at North Parade provided Bathwick with a third river crossing.

Fig. 58 (*above*) 'North Parade Bridge with Pulteney Bridge', photographed by Reverend Francis Lockey 1857. This bridge, designed by W. Tierney Clark in 1835 and constructed of cast iron on stone piers, was once a toll bridge. (*©Bath in Time – Bath Central Library collection*)

Fig. 59 (*below*) North Parade Bridge. (*The Bath & Wilts Chronicle and Herald, 2nd May 1937*)

Fig. 60 (*above*) From *The Bath & Wilts Chronicle and Herald*, August 1936. Work on reconstructing and strengthening the bridge was carried out in 1936. A temporary footpath was built. (*Bath Record Office*)

Fig. 61 (*below*) It was reported by *The Bath & Wilts Chronicle and Herald* on 9th November 1936 that 'The rapid rise of the Avon owing to the heavy rains of the week-end rendered unsafe the temporary footbridge ... (*Bath Record Office*)

In 1838 work started in Henrietta Road which, although a direct route into the city for coaches entering from Cleveland Bridge, was still a rough, unmade extension of Henrietta Street.

On Thursday evening an accident happened, which might have been very serious in its consequences. The Beaufort Coach in coming into Bath, unfortunately upset over a heap of stones which had been incautiously left on the side of the Henrietta Road ...[53]

Fig. 62 Henrietta Villas (c.1895). Most of these Italianate houses were completed by 1856. Several local builders worked on their construction including Samuel Brooks, mason and onetime landlord of the *Alma Tavern* on Sydney Wharf, and George Charmbury Mann, master mason. Mann was a relative of John Vaughan and built many of the Victorian buildings in Bathwick including St. John's Church, the layout of the Smallcombe Vale graveyards and the construction of the mortuary chapels there. (©*Bath in Time – Bath Central Library collection*)

By 1839, the construction of the Great Western Railway saw the Bristol to London mainline push through Bathwick.

The Canal Makes Way for the Railway

As it nears Bath, its original course has been somewhat diverted by the Great Western Railway, with which it runs side by side. The railway being many feet below, has a heavy stone embankment between it and the canal, which embankment having in parts become decayed, has been to a considerable extent cased with brick.[54]

When John Rennie's Kennet & Avon Canal was dug through Bathwick in 1800, it naturally followed the contour of the hillside in a fair sweep of the waterway: from

Fig. 63 'Bathwick', watercolour, c.1830, by an unknown artist. This view was captured before the re-alignment of the waterway. The horse is standing near the place where the 1839 diversion begins. (*©Victoria Art Gallery, Bath & North East Somerset Council*)

Sydney Gardens, along and adjacent to what is now Beckford Gardens and not a great distance from what later became Rockliffe Avenue. By following this line a consistent water level of 120 feet above sea level was achieved and maintained from the top of the Widcombe flight of locks right through to Bradford on Avon.

Although the canal was a massive advance in transport and travel, its success was relatively short-lived due mainly to competition for trade with the Great Western Railway.

The placing of the railway line on the east side of the river and the establishing of the site for Bath Station on the southern side of the city was obviously the most convenient way forward as it provided a fair sweep from the station towards the east.

Furthermore by tunnelling under Bathwick Hill and on through Sydney Gardens, it was possible to maintain a position east of the river and thence through Bathampton meadows and onwards to London. The problem was that at Darlington Wharf the canal stood in the way!

A major engineering feat resulted, the canal being re-aligned by cutting a course further into the hillside which enabled the railway to be laid at a lower level of 95 feet above sea level alongside the waterway. At the same time both are supported by a long graceful retaining wall that starts at Sydney Gardens and finishes at the railway footbridge at the lower end of Hampton Row.

Fig. 64 Hampton Row [Halt]. The halt opened on 18th March 1907 and closed on 29th April 1917. (*Reproduced by Permission of English Heritage, NMR*)

The line also cuts very close to the River Avon at the sharp bend downstream of Grosvenor Bridge and during construction it was necessary for the railway embankment here to be strengthened by another retaining wall and the river bank to be supported by piling. To this day the river bend is known locally as 'Pile Corner'.

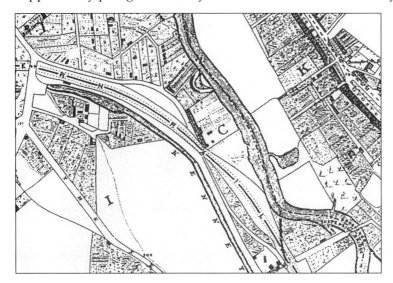

Fig. 65 A section from Cotterell's Map of Bath, 1852. Note the large bend in the river at Grosvenor Bridge and the railway in place. Pile Corner is situated where the parish boundary leaves the river (on the right). (*Bath Record Office*)

It is estimated that well in excess of a million tons of stone and subsoil was removed during construction and most probably went into the building of the railway embankment that runs through Bathampton meadows, whilst surplus material formed the man-made hillock on that side of the boundary at Grosvenor Bridge.

Lighting the Parish

'A beautiful and brilliant light' was the prospect offered by Colonel Pine Coffin, chairman of the Bath Gas Light and Coke Company, in support of a petition for the Act of Parliament that would allow the company to supply coal gas to the city and the parishes of Walcot and Bathwick. There was some opposition, notably from the Bath Commissioners of Police, who thought they should be responsible for supply of gas.[55] But Bath Corporation was keen for streets to be illuminated for the safety of "visitors of quality", and the Gas Light and Coke Company could boast a noted scientist as its superintendent: Dr. Charles Hunnings Wilkinson.[56] The Act was passed in 1818 and the company produced its first gas the same year. In April 1819 the Kingston Rooms had gas lighting for the spring ball. By June 1819 ten miles of main had been laid,[57] and thousands watched the illumination of the City streets on 30th September 1819.

Across the river, the beautiful light dawned a little later. In July 1818 the Bathwick Commissioners, responsible for lighting under the Bathwick Police Act, had placed their usual advertisement for a lamp contractor to fill, light and maintain the parish oil lamps "about 340 in number". (They continued to pay the oil lamp contractor until June 1830.) By 1826 the gas company was estimating the expense of "laying pipes throughout Bathwick parish for the supply of gas for the public lamps" but we know that by 19th May 1829 the gas main had reached no nearer to Sydney Gardens than Johnstone Street, off Laura Place.[58]

Figs. 66 & 67 An early cast-iron lamp post in Sydney Buildings, pictured in July 2007. The base bears the lettering 'Parish of Bathwick' and 'Stothert' (*BLHS Archives*)

That morning an "immense concourse of people" gathered in Sydney Gardens to see aeronaut Charles Green who, in 1821, had made the first manned flight using coal gas, ascend in his "magnificent balloon". This balloon had to be taken first to Johnstone Street to be filled and then back to Sydney Gardens, apparently in tethered flight. It leaked, had to be filled again, finally took off with Green but without an intended passenger – and soon came down in the garden of a house in Kingsmead Terrace.[59] Nevertheless Green went on in 1836 to set a distance record of 480 miles from Vauxhall Gardens to Weilburg in Germany.

In October 1829 the commissioners advertised for a contractor for lighting the public lamps within the Parish of Bathwick

> *for One or more Years from the 29th day of September next ... the Contractor must engage to lay down Main Pipes, Stop Cocks, and all necessary apparatus. The Commissioners to find Pillars and Lanthorns.*

The commissioners had already paid "Mr Stothert" – ironmonger John Stothert – £182 8s on account in December 1828, then £134 13s 7d in 1829. This was probably for lamp posts like the one illustrated above. In 1830 they paid Coles £119 5s for Pillars, Mr Paxton £30 for Lamp Irons, and Francis £20 for fixing Pillars. In February 1831 they paid their first gas bill! Gas "to Dec 25th" cost the parish £162 11s 9d.

St. Mary's by Gaslight

On 25th June 1840 the trustees of St. Mary's asked their clerk to "take the opinion of some eminent Civilian as to whether the Trustees may pay for lighting the Church". Then on 25th July they resolved "that the Church ought to be light with Gas".[60] Their clerk was the solicitor James Frederic Goodridge of Henrietta Street. By 29th July he had drawn up particulars for tenders, "using the present lamps if they can possibly be made available". The work had to be finished by 20th September. The committee received tenders from three "furnishing ironmongers": King & Tuck of Market Place, John Stothert of Northgate Street and George Weedon of Upper Borough Walls. (George Weedon was shown as living at Oak Cottage, Castle Lane, Sydney Gardens in the 1841 *Bath Directory*.) On 10th August John Morris, the committee chairman, signed this memorandum: "Your Committee ... recommend the acceptance of the tender sent in by Messrs King & Tuck for the sum of £64 10s." The very next day a contract was signed – by John Stothert!

> *I hereby engage for the sum of £104 to fit up the said Church according to the foregoing specification with the pillars No 3 the pendants No 2 the pillars being made 3ft 6in high, to provide the lobby & vestry lights to connect the metre with the Main pipe in the Street, to find ground glass shades to make the same fittings complete in every respect for use by the 20 Sept next & to keep the same in repair for Two years from completion, the 20 old Lamps Brackets Chains etc now in the Church to belong to me.*

Why did Goodridge ignore the committee's choice? Certainly, John Stothert was a parishioner, and his children George, Helen, Caroline and Emily had been baptised at St. Mary's in 1833, 1834, 1836 and 1839. Furthermore, Goodridge and Stothert were acquainted: both were city councillors, and Stothert was one of the Bathwick Commissioners for lighting, pitching, paving and cleansing. Goodridge, as clerk, was at their monthly meetings at the Bathwick Hill police station. However, it is likely that Goodridge took advice as to who would do a proper job with gas. He had only to turn to his elder brother, Henry Edmund Goodridge, who used a Henrietta Street address for his architectural practice, although he lived in splendour on Bathwick Hill at *Montebello*, now called *Bathwick Grange*, or may have asked his father James (nearby at No.18 Daniel Street) for advice.

In December 1840 Stothert submitted his bill for £104. It was not paid promptly. There is no record of any replies to Stothert's letters of reminder:

Fig. 68 John Stothert (1792-1879), a Bathwick resident for half a century.
(Bath Record Office)

"I am considerably the loser by the undertaking" and later,

> Will you be so kind as to lend me a Bathwick Police Act for a few hours & will you
> further oblige me by calling a church committee that I may be paid for the gas ...
> More than £20 may have been expended beyond the Estimates.

At last, in the following May the subcommittee appointed to superintend the gas fittings reported that "Mr John Stothert has completed his contract & we consider him entitled to payment accordingly." Sadly, as the century went on, St. Mary's wall decorations suffered from the flaring gas jets and the impurity of the coal gas of those days – "so lethal to Victorian church wall-painting" in the words of the Reverend Richard Prentice. Incandescent gas mantles (which to this day cast a brilliant light on the bar of *The Pulteney Arms*) were not invented until 1885.

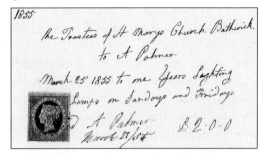

Fig. 69 Receipt for payment of £2 for lighting lamps in St. Mary's Church for one year 1855. This might have been for both oil and gas. (*Somerset Record Office, D/P/batw.m4/2/1*)

John Stothert (1792-1879) was the first child born to the second marriage of George Stothert, founder of the firm that later became Stothert and Pitt. John's half-brother (also named George) already owned the foundry when their father's will was proved in 1819, leaving to John and his brother, William, the ironmonger's business at No.11 Northgate (which now lies beneath the shops on the south side of the Podium).[61] There was also a Stothert yard and warehouse at Sydney Wharf.

The two brothers advertised themselves as Messrs Stothert "furnishing ironmongers to His Majesty" and they manufactured such things as planes, grates and ranges in addition to selling them. An announcement in the *Chronicle* said that Messrs Stothert had purchased land in Bristol for a railway locomotive factory. Under Henry Stothert, John's younger brother, this factory went on to build the locomotives *Arrow* and *Dart*, used in 1840 for the opening of the Bath-Bristol section of the Great Western Railway. In 1844 John and Henry were among nine partners who bought the Cwm Celyn and Blaina Iron Company in Monmouthshire for £77,000. So John had prospered, with continuing financial involvement in the foundry side of the family business. By the time he installed gas at St. Mary's his fellow ironmonger, William, had retired and John was on his own. In 1842 he took Thomas Walker into partnership; then between 1856 and 1858 he sold out of the business. On later census returns he was described as mechanical engineer.

John Stothert had moved to Bathwick after his marriage to Susanna Kelson in 1824, living at No.12 Church Street (now called Raby Place). By 1830 they had moved to a large villa at No.23 Bathwick Hill, opposite *Priory Lodge*. In 1851 this was so full of their children – they had ten in all – that there was no room for servants to live in. In 1879, during the final months of John Stothert's long life, the *Bath Chronicle* was carrying reports of "Thomas Edison's electric light". At St. Mary's, the pendants projecting from the gallery fronts were converted from gas to electricity in 1905.

Smallcombe Vale Cemeteries

In 1851, according to the census, the population count for Bathwick was 5,161, although this figure applies only to people who were present in the parish on census night and does not take into account those normally here but absent at that time.

The pressure on the church authorities to cater for the ever increasing demand for burial spaces within the parish remained undiminished despite extension to the old churchyard adjoining Henrietta Road and Bathwick Street in 1809 and it was therefore agreed that a new burial ground had to be found.

In the event they were assisted in this decision by Acts of Parliament during the period 1852 to 1854: one forbade further burials within metropolitan boundaries and the other, the Public Works Loan Act, made finance available to parishes towards the cost of establishing new graveyards. The Duke of Cleveland, approached for assistance, agreed to make land available adjoining a portion of glebe land in Smallcombe Vale under affordable terms.

Fig. 70 St. Mary the Virgin Churchyard and Mortuary Chapel, Smallcombe Vale.
(*Somerset Record Office, D/P/batw.m2/9/6*)

These two cemeteries comprise the St. Mary the Virgin churchyard, which was laid out on the glebe land[62] and opened in 1856, and a Nonconformists' burial ground, which opened in 1862 on neighbouring land. They are separated by a line of stones stretching from the boundary wall that skirts the edge of Smallcombe Wood, down to the entrance gates below (*see Fig. 78*). During the class-conscious Victorian years these graveyards were simply called the 'Bathwick Cemeteries', although the Church of England churchyard was often referred to as 'the private cemetery' and the Nonconformist as 'the public one'.

The cornerstone of the Church of England chapel was laid in May 1855 using a silver trowel in accordance with the custom at the time and a sovereign, shilling and penny were deposited in a cavity beneath it. The brass plate covering the stone bore the inscription:

The first stone of the burial chapel was laid May 9 1855 by James Brymer Esq of Pulteney Street, Bath, the Rev H.M. Scarth, rector of the parish, Joseph Lansdown and William Thompson, church-wardens, Thomas Fuller, architect and George Mann, builder.[63]

This was an important ceremony in the life of the parish attended by the Rector, Reverend Harry Mengden Scarth, clergy, churchwardens and local dignitaries. Everyone walked in procession from the church to the ground accompanied by parishioners and "a large body of schoolchildren who, at the ceremony, chanted the 119th Psalm followed by the 127th ..."

Fig. 71 (*above*) Burial Fees for 1856.
(*Bath Record Office*)

The ground was later consecrated on 15th February 1856 by the Bishop of Bath and Wells and on 9th March the first burial took place, of John Strut Brown, aged 50. A bird and animal preserver at No.15 Pulteney Bridge, he also ran *The Hampton Museum* at No.14 Hampton Row for many years.

Fig. 72 (*left*) The first burial in the graveyard. 'Sacred to the Memory of John Brown, Naturalist of this City, who died March 9th 1856 aged 50.' (*BLHS Archives*)

Poignantly in the same year the Reverend Scarth's ten-year-old son, Thomas Henry Hamilton Scarth, was the fifth burial, on 30th April.

The Non-Conformist cemetery was first planned in 1858[64] and the land purchased in 1860 by a loan of £1,200 raised from the Public Loans Commissioners[65] to cover all costs. The ground, consisting of an acre and a half of field and woodland to the west of the church's graveyard, was consecrated in January 1861 and opened for burials soon afterwards. Its octagonal mortuary chapel was designed by Alfred Samuel Goodridge. The cemetery layout here is based on a grid system similar to that of St. Mary's, although some of the original walkways have since been given over to accommodate more burials. This graveyard also holds a large proportion of the poorer inhabitants of Bathwick, many of whom are buried in unmarked graves, including infants who were laid to rest around its perimeter. This possibly accounts for a general lack of gravestones in the area when in fact this graveyard is as crowded as the adjacent one.

Among the thousands of people buried in the Smallcombe Vale graveyards are a number of well-known and noteworthy people.

Anthony Beaufort Brabazon MD – a descendant of the House of Brabazon, Co. Meath in Ireland, he entered the medical profession from Trinity College Dublin and went on to tend the wounded at Scutari during the Crimean War. On moving to Bath he took over a medical practice at No.12 Darlington Street from John Kilvert in 1861, on the latter's death. He later became senior physician at the Bath Mineral Water Hospital, then Medical Officer for Health for Bath. He was also senior churchwarden at St. Mary's Church. Dr. Brabazon died on 13th March 1896 aged 75. In addition to a large number of mourners on foot, his funeral was attended by a procession of almost 50 horse-drawn carriages.

Fig. 73 (*left*) The Brabazon grave: In Most Loving Memory of Anthony Beaufort Brabazon MD ... Born 1st August 1820. Died 13th March 1896. This large Celtic cross is decorated with shamrocks and also bears the names of Dr. Brabazon's wife, Eleanor, and several of their children. (*BLHS Archives*)

Fig. 74 (*right*) Portrait of Anthony Beaufort Brabazon MD. (*Bath & County Graphic, 1896*)

George Vincent Fosbery VC (1832-1907) – as a lieutenant in the 4th Bengal Regiment, Indian Army, he was awarded the Victoria Cross for his daring and gallant conduct in recapturing the Crag picket during the Umbeyla Expedition in the North West Frontier of India on 30th May 1863. Fosbery retired from the Army as Lieutenant Colonel in 1877 and from then on devoted himself to the perfecting of machine guns, being the first to introduce them to the British Government. In 1895 he patented a revolutionary semi-automatic, self-cocking revolver which still bears his name. George Fosbery and his wife Emmeline had ten children, many of whom had emigrated to Canada by the time he died on 8th May 1907 whilst on a

Fig. 75 Although not attributed specifically to him, this wooden Cross marks the grave of George Vincent Fosbery VC. The inscription says simply *P.V.Fosbery Psalm 23*. (*BLHS Archives*)

visit to his nephew in Gay Street, Bath. In 1997 his Victoria Cross medal, which had lain in a Canadian vault for decades, was sold at auction in Red Deer, Alberta, Canada for $45,000.

Frederick (Fred) Edward Weatherly KC (1848-1929) – although a barrister and circuit judge by profession, he is today remembered as the popular lyricist who, among his many songs, wrote the words for *Roses of Picardy* and, more famously, *Danny Boy*. For over ten years he lived at No.10 Edward Street where he had the extremely prominent bay window installed. Towards the end of his life he moved, with his second wife Miriam, to No.1 Bathwick Hill where he died on 7th September 1929.

Herbert and Cynthia Asquith – in 1910 Herbert Asquith, known to friends as 'Beb' and son of the Prime Minister Herbert Henry Asquith, married Cynthia Charteris, daughter of Lord Elcho. In 1946 they moved to *Claverton Lodge*, Bathwick Hill, where Beb died a year later in August 1947. Cynthia used to walk across the fields to visit Beb's grave. She liked living on Bathwick Hill, calling the view over Smallcombe Vale down to the lights of the city "a dream of beauty", and stayed at *Claverton Lodge* until her death in 1960 aged 77.

In 1907 the churchyard was extended towards the head of Smallcombe Vale, the land being acquired from Captain Forester, who by then had inherited the Bathwick Estate.

Fig. 76 Side by Side – the matching head stones of Herbert Asquith, died 1947, and Cynthia, his wife, died 1960. (*BLHS Archives*)

Fig. 77 The Nonconformists' burial ground. The Chapel was designed by Alfred Samuel Goodridge in 1861. (*Somerset Record Office D/P/batw.m2/9/6*)

In 1947 Bath Corporation assumed overall responsibility for both graveyards – with the exception of a number of 'Trust graves'[66] – and by 1988 St. Mary's churchyard was deemed full and became an officially closed churchyard[67] by order of HM Queen Elizabeth II in Council.

The caretaker's lodge was sold into private ownership in the 1970s. In 1991 the mortuary chapel was made redundant and is also now privately owned.

St. John the Baptist Church

In an "address to the labouring poor" in 1856, the Rector of Bathwick spoke of his grief that "very few of you have attended the parish church".[68] He had determined to open the chapel in the burial ground off Bathwick Street for a service every Sunday afternoon "to provide for those who plead as an excuse that they have not proper clothes, or that

they cannot hear, or are too infirm to attend a long service". The chapel was probably unheated, and in November 1857 these afternoon services were transferred to St. Mary's for the winter.

There were few free seats at St. Mary's, since pews had been sold freehold to help to pay for the high cost of its building. As the Rector put it,

> *The seats of the poorer class being placed behind the pulpit and reading desk has*
> *placed them at a great disadvantage both as to hearing and seeing.*

The 1861 census showed that the population of Bathwick had continued to increase, and the Rector's analysis was that

> *upwards of 2,000 persons may be reckoned to be of a humble condition of life.*
> *Of the remaining 3,000 and upwards, by far the larger proportion consists of the*
> *families of the gentry; the proportion of trades people being comparatively small.*[69]

By 1861 one of the two curates of the parish, the Reverend Leveson Russell Hamilton (brother-in-law of the Rector), had agreed to pay for the building of a small church to hold about 300. Lord William Powlett had given the ground and promised £100 a year to endow the church. At first it was intended that 270 seats would be free for the labouring poor and 30 let, but in the end all the seats were free.

The cornerstone for St. John the Baptist Church was laid on 24th June 1861. The architect was Charles Edward Giles, who designed a number of Somerset churches around this time, including St. Peter's at Draycott, All Saints at East Clevedon, and St. Michael's at Monkton Combe. The contractor was George Charmbury Mann of No.17 Henrietta Street, who had in 1856 laid out the Smallcombe cemetery and built its first mortuary chapel. The 1861 census shows him as employer of 30 masons, 19 labourers and 6 boys. For building this first St. John's he was paid £2,073.

The architect's impression shows a tower which was not at first completed. The church is depicted as if at road level, making it look grander than it actually was at this stage. One commentator said that the church looked almost toy-like nestled among the trees.

Consecration by the bishop took place on 31st July 1862. Next day, the Reverend Hamilton addressed a meeting of the labouring classes, held in the Rotunda of Sydney Gardens.

I cannot say that the proposal of this new church has been received with any favour or encouragement by the people. They have viewed it with a kind of sullen suspicion.

Fig. 79 (*above*) St. John the Baptist Church. Architect's drawing, 1861. (*By kind permission of the Rector and Churchwardens of St. John's Church, Bathwick*)

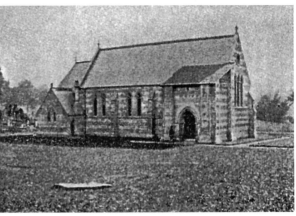

Fig. 80 (*right*) Little St. John's, c.1861. (*By kind permission of the Rector and Churchwardens of St. John's Church, Bathwick*)

Just a year later a newspaper spoke of "crowded and earnest congregations" – though many of these people came across the river from the city. In 1865 a subscription was raised to build the tower and spire, which were completed by November that year at a cost of £600.

"The heat and heaviness of the overcrowded church in those days were both oppressive to the senses and cheering to the heart." So wrote a correspondent to *The Weekly Churchman*.

> We remember a particularly energetic and useful personage, the more worthy successor of the fee-taking Bath pew-opener. Her power of organisation was stretched when a festival attracted a larger congregation than usual. The choir came in singing from the tower door on great days, in order to add dignity to the function. To each bench end was fixed a hinged bracket, which with the chairs completely filled the centre passage. Miss Powell's word of command was 'Now then, ladies and gentlemen, chairs up, brackets down.' Then the seething mass of humanity made themselves and their chairs as small as unvarying bulk would permit, while the choir made a sinuous progress to the chancel.

By 1868 it was clearly necessary to enlarge the church to seat 600. The architect chosen was Arthur Blomfield (later knighted). He retained the low nave of the original church and transformed it into the north aisle by replacing its side wall with pillars and arches. The lofty nave is separated from the raised choir by a stone reredos, and at the east end the sanctuary lies beneath an arch no less than 40 feet high. Blomfield's intended south aisle was not built for reasons of cost. George Mann completed the building work for less than £5,000[70] and the new nave and chancel were consecrated on 9th May 1871.

A month later St. John's became a separate parish with its own vicar. Until this time St. John's had been merely "a chapel of ease" of the parish of Bathwick: for example, it was not licensed to perform marriages. A baptistery with a mosaic floor was added at the west end in 1878.

Fig. 81 Interior of St. John the Baptist Church, c.1946. The Rood, by Sir Ninian Comper, and figures were taken down during the war and put into safe storage. (*By kind permission of the Rector and Churchwardens of St. John's Church, Bathwick*)

The Reverend James Dunn became vicar in September 1879 and served for 40 years, dying at the vicarage in 1919. St. John's became well known for its Anglo-Catholic ritual and Father Dunn came into conflict with the Bishop of Bath and Wells when he insisted that as well as its written law the Church of England had unwritten laws on matters such as fasting.

He was the last of the bishop's "recalcitrant" clergy in that he alone never gave up the use of incense. He was strongly supported by his parishioners: the social mix of the parish had been transformed by the building of the Forester Estate, and the days of "sullen suspicion" were long past.

Fig. 82 Funeral procession of Reverend James Dunn at Raby Place, en route for St. Mary's Churchyard, Smallcombe Vale in June 1919. (*By kind permission of the Rector and Churchwardens of St. John's Church, Bathwick*)

In 1966 the PCC agreed to delete 'the Baptist' from the church title in favour of 'Bathwick St. John'. After the bishop called for a merger of the two Bathwick parishes, the Rector of St. Mary's became priest-in-charge of St. John's in 1976, and then in 1978 vicar of St. John's. Thus came about the United Benefice of Bathwick: St. Mary's and St. John's.

Bathwick Schools

One of the earliest education establishments in Bathwick was Mann's School for Girls, situated in Grove Street in 1809. This early 'free school' is briefly recorded by Dr. James Tunstall during his walks around Bath and appears to have existed at a time when many middle class children were educated at home by a governess or in boarding schools. Most working class and poor children received little or no education except that provided by the church in Sunday schools such as the one at Argyle Chapel, considered to be the oldest congregational chapel in Bath.

The provision of free elementary education for all children took years to establish. This parish, however, was one of the first in Bath to set up an Anglican Church Parochial school, over 30 years ahead of the Education Act and the establishment of School Boards in Bath in 1870. The process first began in 1838 and the following article appeared in *The Bath Chronicle*:

> *EDUCATION OF THE POOR – It is proposed to establish in the parish of Bathwick, a Parochial School for the instruction of children of both sexes, in connection with the National Society for the Education of the Children of the poor in principles of the Established Church. The want of a school of this kind has long been felt in Bathwick, and it is hoped that the liberal assistance of the friends of religious instruction will be afforded to the proposed establishment. The circular by which the public attention has been invited to this subject, says that "the Parish of Bathwick, although comprising a very large proportion of wealthy inhabitants, yet contains a population of 1400 persons in that class of life to whom a good and suitable education for the youth of both sexes, is at present an advantage beyond their reach, at least without sending their children through the most crowded streets of the city to a distance from their homes. There is, indeed, one small School for girls in the parish, maintained by the casual bounty of a lady, and there has lately been built a School-room for Infants; but it must be manifest that in a population of the above-named amount, there is a necessity for additional means of instruction." His Grace the Duke of Cleveland has granted, as a site for the proposed school, a piece of ground in a central situation, at a merely nominal rent. It is suggested to such persons as have cause of sound Christian education at heart, to give and obtain pecuniary aid for this project, whether they reside in the parish of Bathwick or not.*[71]

Victoria Infants School was built by John Vaughan at a cost of more than £600 and opened in 1839. His fee for the construction was £555 with extra expenses added for overlaying the foundations with sheet iron and also varying amounts of compensation paid to previous occupiers of the land for fruit trees and vegetables lost. The money was raised by subscription but even before completion it was found necessary to enlarge the single-storey, one-roomed building, as its dimensions were inadequate for the reception of the 150 children expected to attend. The plan also included the erection of a teacher's residence and stipulated that the school would be used on weekdays for the education of children of both sexes with those living nearest having preference: "Provided always, that no child shall be admitted to the Week-day School aforesaid after the age of six years, nor retained after the age of seven years" and on Sundays it was to be used "as a Sunday school superintended by the Curate of the Parish of Bathwick."

The children were taught by one teacher and an assistant, provided with pinafores and boots, and given soup at midday. Numbers attending fluctuated from year to year but in 1874 the school had 188 children on its register, 52 of them under the age of four – and all taught in one room!

Fig. 83 Lettering above the door of the former Victoria Infants School building (now residential). (*BLHS Archives*)

The Parochial school in St. John's Road, designed by John Pinch (the younger), cost £1,000 to build and opened its register on 1st February 1841. The children were taught separately, with boys upstairs and girls on the ground floor. By the end of the first year 76 girls aged from six to thirteen were attending. Parents' occupations ranged from blacksmith, lamplighter, brightsmith and wheelwright to hairdresser, nurse, servant, charwoman and washerwoman.

In the early days schooling had to be paid for, and by 1882 the fee for the first child amounted to "threepence and tuppence for every other child from the same family".

Some families were desperately poor and there were always several children sent home because their fees had not been paid. Many of these were ragged and the school regularly appealed for cast-off clothing for them. Children from the orphanage at No.2 Bathwick Street also attended lessons.

Each schoolroom was heated by a single stove and boys were required to 'bring up the coals' whilst the girls laid the fires and swept the classrooms. During lessons in very cold weather the children were allowed to take turns standing nearest the stove.

As the playgrounds were below flood level, flood damage was a regular occurrence and the schools would close for several days.

The first master was named Biggs and the next, Henry Hale, was one of the longest-serving headmasters at the parochial school, where he started his teaching career in 1858, aged 29, and continued until he retired in 1891. He was considered fair in his judgement of both pupils and staff but also had a reputation for being a strict disciplinarian. This was demonstrated in the case of a young pupil teacher who was instantly dismissed for

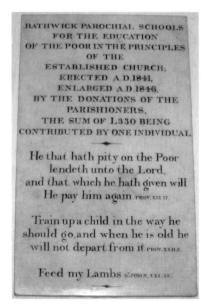

Fig. 84 (*above*) Marble tablet removed from the old school and now in place on the wall of the entrance hall of the present school in Darlington Road. (*Terry Hardick 2006*)

Fig. 85 (*below*) Bathwick Parochial School (designed by John Pinch the younger) pictured in 1999 boarded up and awaiting redevelopment into residential use. (*BLHS Archives*)

Fig. 86 A class at Bathwick Parochial Boys School in 1904. (*Terry Hardick collection*)

Fig. 87 (*left*) Children **at** Bathwick Parochial School, c.1928. The school merged with Victoria Infants School in 1927. This picture shows the range of children from about the age of four to eleven. Note the three boys in smocks (bottom left). Smocks were issued to all the infant children and replaced annually as prizes for good behaviour. (*The Bath Chronicle*)

Fig. 88 Bathwick St. Mary's, 1968 – 40 years on from the above. On the right is Mr Pursey, Headmaster and on the left Miss Folwell. Philip Chant is seen second on the right in the second row. (*Philip Chant collection*)

habitually sending boys during school hours with letters and papers, as well as at times with money to lay bets on Race Horses at the Beefsteak Tavern at the back of the market and frequently to fetch sporting papers for him.[72]

Nineteenth-century school discipline was strict, punishments often severe and the Bathwick schools were no exception. In the parochial school, within a period of 12 weeks from 30th January to 8th May 1893, 28 punishments of 58 strokes of the cane were recorded as given for various misdemeanours, including one to a nine-year-old orphan who was caned for bad handwriting. This turned out to be counterproductive as the child suffered a badly bruised hand and for some weeks was unable to use it! Overall, though, according to the annual Education Inspector's reports, whenever the school was inspected conditions were good, the children were happy and the level of learning high. In 1922 the boys and girls schools amalgamated and joined with Victoria Infants School in 1927.[73]

By 1986 the school had moved to new premises in Darlington Road and the building in St. John's Road was left empty awaiting redevelopment into apartments. The land, originally given under covenant for educational use, has since reverted to the Vane family and all the old school buildings are now fully residential.

The Victorians continued to maintain some of the privately run schools and colleges in the parish set up by their predecessors and also established several of their own. From 1846-1869 a Ladies Seminary and Boarding School occupied No.103 New Sydney Place. This was owned and run by Mrs Frances Drought and catered for a total of nine resident female pupils ranging in age from eight to eighteen who were taught a variety of subjects including English grammar, literature and French. All the inhabitants of the house were female and no men were allowed on the premises, not even a manservant!

Fig. 89 (New) Sydney Place c.1919. Mrs Drought's Ladies' Seminary occupied the large corner house. The seminary was possibly a forerunner of the La Sainte Union Convent School for girls which opened in Pulteney Road in 1857. (*BLHS Archives*)

Young gentlemen were educated at the Bath College in *Darlington Villa*, North Road, which was owned and run by the Reverend Francis Kilvert and his wife Leanora. In 1837 they moved to *Claverton Lodge*, Bathwick Hill where the college continued until about 1854, on the death of the Reverend Kilvert.[74] In 1856 as the Bath Proprietary College (later Sydney College) its governors took over *Sydney Hotel*[75] and continued there until around 1883.

Fig. 90 *Claverton Lodge*, Bathwick Hill, built c.1825. (*Terry Hardick 2007*)

One of the last small preparatory schools in Bathwick was St. Nicholas School at No.21 Great Pulteney Street. This school had been founded by Miss Helen Wills in 1927 at No.4 Darlington Street.[76] The children were given an elementary education by Miss Wills and an assistant, and for recreation the young pupils used to walk in crocodile formation to Sydney Gardens where they played games. When it was time to return to school Miss Wills blew a whistle to assemble the children. Discipline was strict and any child who misbehaved was denied the games time. By 1954 the school had moved to Great Pulteney Street and recreation was taken in Henrietta Park. St. Nicholas School closed in 1974 and Miss Wills died in 1978 aged 83.

Fig. 91 Children of St. Nicholas School, c.1954. Although the front entrance to St. Nicholas House is in Sunderland Street, the postal address was always No.21 Great Pulteney Street. (*Mirella Keyford collection*)

The Folly and Cremorne Gardens

The *Folly Inn* once stood on the edge of the eastern boundary of the parish on a piece of land lying between the canal and the River Avon. Nobody knows the reason for its name though during the 17th and 18th centuries buildings so called were often a wry reference to human folly!

Fig. 92 Section from *Bath from the East, with the Old Folly Inn and GWR,* watercolour (undated) by Samuel Poole, 1870-1947. (©*Victoria Art Gallery, Bath & North East Somerset Council*)

The ground is depicted on the 1727 map as 'No.31 garden' indicating that it was once cultivated land and although not shown, a property is known to have existed there at that time. A later map of 1770[77] shows the plot complete with a substantial building facing the river and by 1786 this was called the 'Folly'.

> BATHWICK *Whereas the River in the Manor of Bathwick, extending from Dolemeads to the Folly, now rented by me has been frequently robbed of Fish. I do hereby give notice, that whoever shall in future fish without my permission, or commit any trespass on that part of the River, shall be proceeded against as the law directs.*
>
> *Richard Pearce.*[78]

At this time Richard Pearce rented the entire piscatorial rights of the River Avon within the boundaries of Bathwick although the length of his tenancy is not known.

The same building also appears on Harcourt Masters' *Plan of Bath* of 1795 where it is shown to be well sited just above the bend in the river and commanding a view downstream towards Camden Crescent and the city. Early access to the place was obtained by means of a 'free ferry'[79] across the river from Grosvenor and trackways across fields from the Hampton Way. A footpath also ran directly to the boundary along the river bank from the old village.

By 1799 the Folly land was leased to William Hulbert, yeoman and dairy farmer and from then on it remained in the ownership of successive members of the Hulbert family for several more decades.

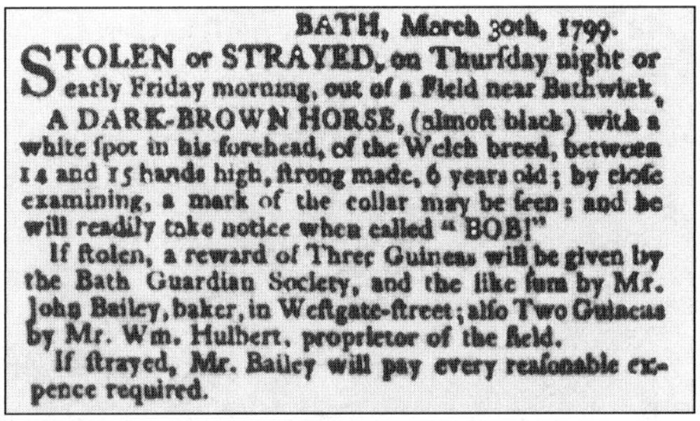

In 1838 as the laying of the Great Western Railway Paddington to Bristol line was in progress, part of the land occupied by the Folly lay in its path, although the actual building and its immediate precincts were unaffected.

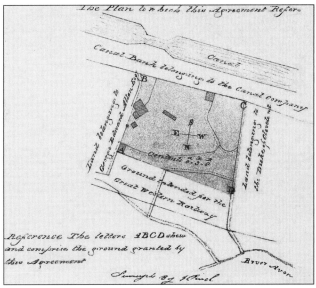

Fig. 93 From *The Bath Journal*, 1799. (*Bath Central Library*)

The Railway Company then acquired, by compulsory purchase, a large section of the area including the whole of the Folly land and the subsequent construction of the railway embankment meant that the view of the river from the house was totally destroyed.

Well over 50 per cent of the ground was taken over for the railway including the 17½ metres of river frontage. A diverted Right of Way still runs from Hampton Row through the old Folly grounds to Grosvenor Bridge (built 1836) which together with a small triangular plot of land on the railway side of the path is now all that is left of the curtilage of the original farm.

During the re-alignment of the canal in 1839 the Folly site was redeveloped[80] and although William Hulbert and his son Matthew William Jones Hulbert continued with dairy farming on their remaining land, the garden became a 'tea gardens' run by Mrs Mary Hulbert (wife of Matthew).

William Hulbert died in 1845 aged 88 years followed in 1847 by his son aged 56 and the farm then passed to William Henry (son of Matthew and Mary) who carried on the family farming tradition for several more decades.

By 1850 the Folly tea gardens was also advertised as a licensed beerhouse and in 1861, Mr Thomas Osmond, landlord of *The Theatre Tavern* in Bath, took over the lease of the *Folly Tavern*, the Hulberts moving to Hampton Row where they had more property.

Fig. 94 Plan from the 'Agreement for Re-building on Folly Ground, His Grace the Duke of Cleveland and Matthew William Jones Hulbert, 10th June 1839', surveyed by J. Pinch [the younger]. (*Bath Record Office*)

Osmond expanded and developed the Folly into the 'Cremorne Pleasure Gardens' of Bathwick,[81] a venture that appears to have been an economic success. However, complaints made to the Bath Corporation from residents living in the vicinity regarding rowdy revellers returning home along the canal towpath and also bathing in the canal suggest that the gardens were not viewed favourably by everyone![82] Such behaviour could not be tolerated in Victorian Bathwick and the Watch Committee was obliged to act

that a sergeant accompanied by a constable should give account for not interfering with the nuisance and directed that the police see that such bathing took place no earlier than at nine o'clock in the evening.

The enterprise of Cremorne Pleasure Gardens lasted until 1885 when Thomas Osmond withdrew and invested his fortune, rather unwisely, in a South American Railway Company in territory where perpetual revolution had become rife!

Fig. 95 Thomas Osmond (undated). (*Bath Record Office, Acc 418*)

The premises then returned to its previous use as an inn with a brewery attached, but over the following years few tenant landlords remained for very long.

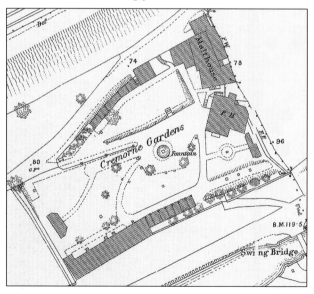

Fig. 96 Section from the 1886 OS map showing Cremorne Gardens in detail.

Fig. 97 (*above*) Tokens: (*top*) obverse Folly, reverse Hulbert; (*bottom left*) Castle Tavern; (*bottom right*) T. Osmond, Cremorne, Bath. (©*Bath in Time – Private collection, Bath*)

The last time that the inn was commercially occupied was on the night of 26th April 1942 during the Bath Blitz in the Second World War when a stray bomb landed in the garden and exploded in a large tree. Although the blast blew in the doors and windows it apparently did little structural damage and the building remained standing. A local

ARP (Air Raid Precautions) warden, Dan Hardick, who was on duty at the time dealing with a small outbreak of fire in the dead long grass, probably ignited by a tracer bullet fired from one of the German planes, heard the all too characteristic whistle made by a falling bomb and was saved from injury by falling flat on the ground just before the explosion. It was Dan's duty to inspect the premises to assess casualties, arrange evacuation, report what level of accommodation the survivors would need and also record the names of those in the building, but although this event took place in the early hours of the morning, at about 1.40am, he discovered that the public bar had been packed at the time of the explosion. Fortunately no one had been injured in any way. Dan, however, found himself in rather an awkward situation as under the licensing laws of the day the premises should have closed at 10.30pm the previous evening and there was clearly a breach of the law! Nevertheless he made his list and assured all those present that he would be returning on the following morning with details of alternative accommodation. However upon his return a short time later the premises were totally deserted and all stocks and removable assets gone including the landlord!

After this memorable event the *Folly Tavern* was never to see occupation again and rapidly fell into a state of ruin. Over time materials were progressively looted and whatever remained was gradually absorbed into the undergrowth. Today the site is thick woodland and the only trace to be found of past habitation is a side retaining wall to the garden and a crumbling flight of ivy-covered steps.

The Boating Station
The boating station premises stretch across land that is depicted on William Pulteney's map of 1727 as 'The Ennix and Frize Moor', though by early 1800 this ground became known as part of Villa Fields.

Fig. 98 The Boating Station at Bathwick, c.1900. (*Terry Hardick collection*)

Although the year that the boating station was firmly established is unclear, from the meagre evidence available it was certainly in existence by 1833, just a few years after the opening of the new (Cleveland) bridge in 1827. A ferry is known to have existed in that vicinity for many years and it is thought that a displaced ferryman whose livelihood had become redundant as a result of the new bridge may then have moved the short distance upriver to operate near or on the site of the present boating station.

Although not proven, a story handed down over the years of the boatyard's history tells of the beaching of the original ferry boat near here and the theory is further supported by the discovery a few years ago of 18th-century boat fittings on this land.

In 1833 James Aust, a gardener, held the tenancy of the site from the Manorial estate and by 1841 he was offering "new boats built new and for sale and also for public hire." The business then became known as Aust's Pleasure Gardens and highly competitive boat races between the Bath City Police Force and the Fire Brigade took place on this stretch of the river.

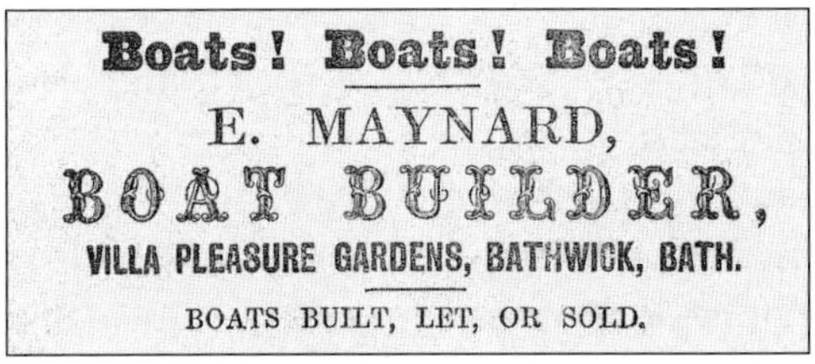

James Aust died in 1848 and it is believed that his son remained as tenant of the site until 1861 when Ernest Maynard took over and the premises became known as Maynard's Boating Station (or occasionally as the 'Cleveland Boating Station'), where boat building and public hire of boats apparently flourished in the ensuing years.

Boats! Boats! Boats!

E. MAYNARD,

BOAT BUILDER,

VILLA PLEASURE GARDENS, BATHWICK, BATH.

BOATS BUILT, LET, OR SOLD.

Fig. 99 Advertisement from the *Bath Directory*, 1862.

Prior to the turn of that century Charles Maynard, possibly Ernest's son, terminated the tenancy in order to re-establish himself in the same trade on the River Thames at Windsor but he later returned to Bath for his closing years. On his death his ashes, as he had requested, were scattered on the river here.

The Bath Boating Company Limited, formed when Maynard left, then appointed Fred Fisher as its manager and he and his family took up residency in the cottage in the grounds. Fisher had first started work in the boatyard in 1876 at the age of 13 and knew the trade well. Business flourished as the Edwardians continued to show an

an interest in boating, especially in competitive rowing and soon several Bath rowing clubs occupied the picturesque riverside clubhouses at the station. This success meant that by about 1911 Fred was in a position to purchase the business complete with assets and

Fig. 100 Fred Fisher (right) at the Boating Station, c.1900. (*Terry Hardick collection*)

able to trade under his own name although he remained as the leaseholder with the Bathwick Estate Company as his landlord until 1921[83] when he secured his freehold for the sum of £1,400. The premises then comprised 1¼ acres of land with 200 yards of river frontage and the cottage, plus rowing clubrooms, workshops and boat sheds.

Over the years there were various problems, including flooding which caused damage to both the wooden buildings and stock, but the business survived. 130 years after Fred Fisher started work at the Boating Station the business remains in the hands of his descendants. Today traditional boat building is carried out in much the same way as it was during the Victorian and Edwardian years although the business concentrates mainly on boating for pleasure.

St. John's Road

Memories of St. John's Road indicate that at first it was a leafy lane, with but a few old cottages on either side dotted among gardens, orchards and smallholdings.

Leading from Cleveland Bridge to Grove Street, by 1880 it was known as Henrietta Lane. As the lane approached Grove Street it passed the Bathwick Schools, Henrietta Buildings and several houses of the late Victorian period. The houses survive and the school buildings are now residential but Henrietta Buildings has since been demolished and as the road bends around past the school, a notable landmark that

Fig. 101 A section of St. John's Road, c.1880. (*By kind permission of the Rector and Churchwardens of St. John's Church, Bathwick*)

once stood just beyond it has also disappeared. This was a large, mature mulberry tree that bore abundant fruit on branches extending across the roadway which abruptly narrows here.

The 1886 Ordnance Survey Map depicts the new road, now with St. John's Church at one end, complete with pavements, street lighting and fire point. The earliest mention of the road's present name is in 1884 when John Marshman, butcher and tripe dresser, became the first to advertise in the *Bath Post Office Directories* as being situated in "St John's road". Marshman also had a slaughterhouse attached to his two-storey building here, although in later years the premises took on the more desirable name of *Fern Bank*!

One of the oldest dwellings in St. John's Road was *The Rosery* which stood in a large orchard of pear trees of an impressive size that stretched down to the river at the

Fig. 102 *The Rosery* in St. John's Road, c.1938. The date of construction of this cottage is unknown but a dwelling was present on this site before 1838. Pictured are Mrs Rosetta Hardick (left) and a family friend. The Hardick family occupied the cottage from about 1900-1950 and once built a boat – inside the cottage. When finished, a window and a large part of the exterior wall had to be demolished to get the vessel out. However, by the middle of the night all had been restored! (*Terry Hardick collection*)

back and at the front faced a narrow track which led to another cottage and garden a few yards further on. For many years *The Rosery* and adjoining ground was occupied by Henry Griffen, organ builder, and his family.

Later the site became the yard and offices belonging to a local builder, F.J. Amery & Sons Ltd who also had premises in Grove Street. Building materials such as bricks and concrete blocks were stored beneath the pear trees and during the harsh years of the depression in the 1920/30s this local firm was among the few that managed to survive without making any of their best craftsmen redundant. They did this by prudently investing their capital in developing their land and in doing so built most of the pre-war houses that line the road today.

In 1920 St. John's Road consisted of 14 two-storeyed houses, a detached two-storeyed house, two schools with garden and playground, a coal yard and carpenter's shop, two two-storeyed cottages (one with a slaughterhouse attached – ex Marshman's land) and various other plots of gardens and small workshops. By 1938 the road was still a mix of houses, local industry, garages and business premises. For postal delivery purposes these were numbered from 7 to 81.

Fig. 103 The lane between the back of St. John's Road and Henrietta Villas, c.1965. The dog's name was 'Smog'. (*John and Jo Marsh collection*)

On the eastern side of the road, a short distance from the school, stood Whitings Motor Garage. This was a single-storey building of utility quality and during the 1939/45 war the premises were occupied by the Admiralty with an armed guard always on duty. Also during the war as the Government-planned scheme 'Dig for Victory' got underway and the search for land for food production became more urgent, the

Fig. 104 The rear of St. John's Road c.1965. The garage and workshops of Bodywork Ltd. (*John and Jo Marsh collection*)

adjacent piece of ground now occupied by *Vulcan House* (built 1959), was laid out as allotments. St. John's Church Rooms were also used extensively during the war, often as classrooms for children evacuated from East London to the Bathwick and Walcot area.

During the last years of the 20th century further development took place and today St. John's Road is almost entirely residential.

Figs. 105 & 106 (*above and left*) Demolition of the workshops for the development of Minerva Court (built in 1987). (*John and Jo Marsh collection*)

Sham Castle Lane and Vellore Lane

Eastwards on the opposite side of the parish from St. John's Road lie Sham Castle Lane and Vellore Lane. This area was also largely untouched by Georgian development and remained as orchards and gardens with a few small cottages and smallholdings until well into the 20th-century postwar years.

The original lines of both lanes are ancient and stretch back at least as far as the Roman occupation. In 1727 this area was known as No.109, Beech Tree Ground[84] and the distinctive outline of this land can still be traced today.

One of the oldest remaining buildings is *Windsor Cottage*, which was owned and occupied in early 1800 by William Henry Marks who leased other property and land in the area which he then let out. Opposite *Windsor Cottage*, overlooking the canal and Sydney Wharf, stood another old building occupied by Marks' son, Matthew Henry Marks, a cabinet maker and brewer who made and sold beer and cider on the premises. At this time much of Matthew Marks' trade probably came from the hauliers and carters travelling up and down Sham Castle Lane and Vellore Lane en route to the canal from the quarries and by 1841 the brewhouse was known as 'Castle Tavern, near Canal Office, Sydney Gardens'.

During the construction of the railway through Bathwick canal traffic was seriously disrupted, sending trading on Sydney Wharf into a decline from which it never fully recovered. Shortly after 1841, although Matthew Marks's brewery was still present in Sham Castle Lane, there is no mention of the *Castle Tavern* on the canal bank. A short distance away at Villa Fields, however, in an area where hundreds of thirsty navvies and carters were digging out the rail line, a newly-built *Windsor Castle* was in business! This building was later rebuilt and is known today as *The Castle*, Forester Avenue.

William Marks senior died in 1849 aged 83 and *Windsor Cottage* then became the home and business premises of his son-in-law, Benjamin Cantle, a fly carriage owner. Meanwhile Matthew Marks had enlarged his premises into *Castle Villa* and this building appears to have survived into the 1920s after which it became a ruin and was eventually demolished.

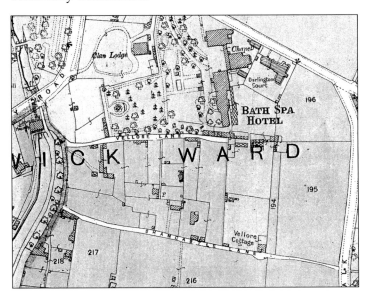

Fig. 107 Bathwick 1919 showing Sham Castle Lane and Vellore Lane. Note at the bottom of Sham Castle Lane is *Windsor Cottage* and next to the short track (No.218) is *Castle Villa* (once *Castle Tavern*). Note also *Bath Spa Hotel* and *Vellore Cottage*. (*BLHS Archives*)

Another old building that survives in Sham Castle Lane is *Vellore Cottage*. The present building was constructed in 1866 but there are records of an earlier dwelling on this site before 1840. The cottage takes its name from *Vellore House*, later the *Bath Spa Hotel*.

Vellore House has had many uses over the years. It was built in 1835 for Colonel Augustus Andrews who named it after the garrison town of Vellore in India where he was once stationed. Later it became the residence of the Reverend Charles Kemble, Rector of Bath Abbey, and in 1878 was taken over as The Bath College for Boys. This closed in 1909, after which the building became a hotel. Haile Selassie, the exiled Emperor of Ethiopia, stayed here in 1936. During the war years, 1939-45, when the building and grounds had been requisitioned by the Admiralty, Winston Churchill would visit occasionally for high-level meetings.

The stables and outbuildings of *Vellore House* once backed onto Vellore Lane, a short narrow road where a few small dwellings with gardens and hothouses also stood. The stables and outbuildings are now converted for other uses and Vellore Lane is quietly residential.

Fig. 109 Aerial view taken on 2nd August 1945. Note the two sets of long buildings on the left of the picture. These are in the grounds of *Bath Spa Hotel*, a property which has had many identities over the years. During the 1939-1945 war it was used by the Admiralty when the long shed-like buildings were erected. After the war the house became a nurse's home but later was turned back into a hotel once again. (*English Heritage, NMR – RAF Photography*)

Henrietta Park

For centuries this low-lying part of the Bathwick mead was open flood plain. It was a popular place to walk and picnic and an ancient footpath led past the mill on the river bank at Spring Gardens towards the ferry and the city beyond.

By 1795 an ambitious plan was devised for a square (Frances Square) to link up with the main thoroughfares of Bathwick Street, Great Pulteney Street and eventually Upper Great Pulteney Street. The plan came to nothing. Neither Frances Square nor Upper Great Pulteney Street was constructed and most of the meadow land remained untouched by development until 1840 when, divided into two fields still browsed by livestock and encompassed by roads, it was known as Bathwick Park. By 1860 these fields had become 'Henrietta Park', "family associations replacing the local designation ...", where local cricket and football clubs often played inter-parish games. From 1892 to 1894 Bath Rugby Club used the fields, their last game here being in September 1895. The park was also a sports ground for boys from Sydney College.

In 1895 Captain Forester offered the seven acres of Henrietta Park to the City of Bath with the proviso

> that it should be dedicated and laid out as a public park ... and should remain an open space and never be built upon ...[85]

The offer was unanimously accepted by the Bath Corporation Pleasure Grounds Committee and in October of that year estimates were obtained for

> cutting and stacking turf, 2955 yards super ...
> Excavating to an average depth of 8 ins after removal of 657 yards cubic ...
> Excavating 12 cesspits 3ft 0ins x 6ft 0ins at 1/6d per yard cubic ...

also removal of the existing path through the centre and re-erection of a

> flag staff 600ft x 2ft 3ins ...

SUMMARY OF ESTIMATES

Iron Fencing	£ 40.0.0
Forming paths &c, as above	£161.7.0
bandstand, to include foundation and base in stone ..	£20.0.0
Work to wall in Henrietta Street and extra railings ..	£10.0.0
Gardener's tool house, and urinal drain, &c	£30.0.0
Add for unseen incidentals	£20.0.0

These estimates excluded plants and by February 1896 it was decided to limit costs: "For laying out and planting not to exceed £500." Annual maintenance was put at £100. The figures quoted were not accepted by the councillors who pressed for "a scheme of less expensive character", whereby a revised estimate of £375 was offered and agreed. This consisted of architect's commission, seats, lawn mower, plants and annual maintenance costs of £75 but omitted the bandstand and gardener's tool shed.

By July 1896 tenders were advertised, with a contract of completion of work within five weeks of 1st September, but the actual official opening date was to be delayed to coincide with Queen Victoria's Jubilee celebrations in June 1897.

Local opposition to the plan related mainly to restriction of access to the ground and its ancient 'Rights of way' and this was dealt with by an instruction issued to the Pleasure Grounds Committee *to refrain from obstructing or diverting the Public Pathway through Henrietta Park without previously obtaining legal sanction ...*

However the committee did not agree and concluded

that the path was not a highway, and therefore the Authority had the power to close it without obtaining an order from the Court of Quarter Sessions ... Captain Forester was quite within his legal rights to close it ... that the committee had gone back to 1842 when this property forming part of the Bathwick Estate was a strict settlement, and that nobody was in a position to dedicate it to the public. Captain Forester had, however, obtained a clause in a special Act of Parliament that had enabled him to do so. According to the committee in 1896, although this path had been used by the public for many years they did not have any rights to it and furthermore, for the last fourteen or fifteen years it had been closed. Wilcox (the Waterman) and later George Fisher, had kept the gate chained and locked.

Fig. 110 The park prior to layout c.1895. Note the flag pole and railings. At this time the path was chained and locked at night. (© *Bath in Time – Bath Central Library collection*)

Bathwick streets were decorated with flags, flowers and bunting of red white and blue for the Jubilee celebrations on 22nd June 1897. Pulteney Street was reported to be ablaze with light from end to end with Chinese lanterns and fairy lights, while in Argyle Street, Pert's Dye Works sported a huge portrait of the Queen with a shield underneath bearing the words "We would dye for Ye". Thousands of people attended the event and at 11am amid

the pealing of bells from various church steeples and the occasional boom of a gun "saluting" to one solitary discharge somewhere in the distance ...[86]

the park was transferred to the City of Bath and officially opened as a public amenity by the Mayor, Councillor Woodiwiss. He declared: "the park is open to the use of the Public for ever" and as the speeches ended, a Jubilee Oak tree was planted on the south-east green[87] and a procession of the Mayor, Mace-bearers, Clergy and Councillors

Fig. 111 (*left*) The Opening of Henrietta Park, 22nd June 1897. (*Bath & County Graphic*)

Fig. 112 (*below*) This marble commemoration tablet was once fixed to the wall of a wooden shelter which stood where the public toilets are situated now. (*Terry Hardick 2007*)

accompanied by the fire brigade in full regalia and the Bath Military Band "trod the newly-rolled paths in leisurely state" pausing to read the inscription on the west wall.

The layout of Henrietta Park was copied from Georgian plans and this is seen in the central lawn and circular path of the park which are laid out to match almost exactly the original scheme for the intended square. The central circle of green is surrounded by a series of paths said to total about half a mile which were initially designed to be raised to the level of the surrounding roads. However, as the park lies on a bed of

Fig. 113 Henrietta Park c.1930. (© *Bath in Time – Bath Central Library collection*)

Fig. 114 Bathwick RFC was one of the several sports clubs that used the park. This picture was taken in 1923. Sam Bailey is holding the ball. (*BLHS Archives*)

gravel that in turn rests in a kind of saucer of blue clay which consequently holds a large amount of water, the idea of raising the level of the pathways was not adopted as this would impede drainage. It was generally accepted by then that in times of flood or any sudden rise in the river water table, water collecting in the soil beneath the park would be unable to escape and drainage was therefore provided by means of 15 catchpits, each six feet by three. This system remained in place until the Flood Prevention Scheme of the 1970s.

A 'Home for Strays'

In 1893 a piece of land at the rear of the houses on the west side of Daniel Street and overlooking Henrietta Park, became a shelter for a number of stray dogs. Erected at

Fig. 115 The shelter. "The dogs had a daily run in the country, 3 or 4 stock dogs leading the way" (©*Bath in Time – Bath Central Library collection*)

the cost of £170 for Miss Emily Haigh of Sydney Place, the 'home' accommodated over 50 animals in eight covered pens with railed open enclosures, all built around a central single-storey structure approximately 18 feet square, with lighting and drainage. Adjoining the main building was an infirmary for 20 sick or injured dogs and an exercise yard.

> The 'Home' is situated on the side of Henrietta Park furthest away from the City and in a most healthy and secluded spot. A good caretaker lives on the premises, in the adjoining cottages, he is most assiduous in his attention to the dogs, many of whom are often brought to him in a starving and poor condition ...[88]

The aim of the shelter was to provide the animals with "the comforts of a happy home" where they were kept for three weeks whilst new good homes were found. Their benefactor, Miss Haigh, lived in Sydney Place for many years and the shelter she set up in Bathwick foreshadowed a centre for stray animals that later started up in Greenway Lane, Bath, and went on to become the present Bath Cats and Dogs Home at Claverton Down.

In 1913, because of complaints from local residents, Miss Haigh was given notice of termination of tenancy by Captain Forester, owner of the land, and all traces of the dogs and their home were subsequently cleared away.

The plot of land where the shelter stood is part of what is now called Henrietta Gardens, an area which throughout the previous years of development remained largely untouched until 1919 when during the 'Sale of Bathwick' it was described thus:

> Two Cottages with Ranges of Stabling, Store Sheds, Motor Garage, Engine House and Yard attached. Plots of Garden and Nursery Ground, Builders Yard and Allotments, the whole having extensive Building Frontage overlooking Henrietta Park, and at present let on Yearly Tenancies ... producing Rack Rents aggregating to £69 2s. per annum.

Most of the land was then sold for building and over the following years the present houses were constructed.

Local Traders Serving the Parish

No large factories were ever built in Bathwick and it seems that the old traditions of market gardening, the business of transport and the practice of erecting elegant well- designed buildings generally held firm.

By the end of the 18th century the parish was known to be the favourite resort of some of the 'best families' who visited Bath. Accordingly lodging houses could be found in almost any street.

Throughout the years various shops scattered over three separate areas of Bathwick also served the community, although by 1898 redevelopment at the southern end of Bathwick Street resulted in the loss or alteration of some of them. At this time, during the rebuilding of *The Crown Inn*, the post office was moved across the street where it remained until closure in January 2005. Today only two shops standing within the old parish boundary retain a vestige of their original trade: the chemist's shop in Argyle Street, established before 1826, and a grocery shop in George's Place.

Fig. 116 (*above*) George's Place, Bathwick Hill, 1906. Shops were established here by 1819. A Post Office Receiving-house was present in George's Place from before 1846. P.E. Penny, baker and confectioner was at No. 2 for only a short time in 1906 but the post office business remained until 2001, when as Bathwick Hill Post Office, it finally closed. The dairy (left) is now Bathwick Hill Stores. (*Ken Smith collection*)

Fig. 117 (*below*) J. H. Harding, Bathwick Street, Family Grocers from 1889-1988. In 1898 extensive alterations to all the shop fronts in Bathwick Street were carried out. This picture dates from about 1910. (*John Carson collection*)

During the Victorian period there were also at least 16 public houses in Bathwick, although some of these were very short-lived and today only six remain: *The Boater* (formerly *Argyle Tavern*) in Argyle Street, *The Rising Sun* in Grove Street, *The Pulteney Arms* in Daniel Street, *The Castle* in Forester Avenue and *The Crown* [*Inn*] and *The Barley* [*Mow*] in Bathwick Street.

Industry included the Bath Brewery in Bathwick Street, the Maltsters (later Baird & Sons) at Sydney Buildings and Day & English, Brass & Iron Works in Spring Gardens Road where the two-stroke petrol engine was developed in about 1888.

As the effects of the demise of the Kennet & Avon Canal and later the depression of the early 1900s took hold in Bathwick many local traders went out of business. Some bravely struggled on and motor transport that replaced the horse flourished, though business was very quiet during war years on account of no petrol – or horses!

One of the oldest small Victorian family-run firms still trading in the mid 20th century was John Howard & Sons, Sanitary Engineers and General Builders of Edward Street and Pulteney Mews who were in business from c.1866 until 1968. Howards did a variety of work and in 1907 were contracted to enlarge and lay out an additional section of burial ground in St. Mary the Virgin churchyard at Smallcombe Vale. They also did work for the Bathwick Estate Company and their name can still be seen on old manhole covers and other drain covers around the parish, though modern ones are gradually replacing these. Their showrooms in Argyle Street are now a newsagent and convenience store and the premises in Edward Street/Pulteney Mews residential.

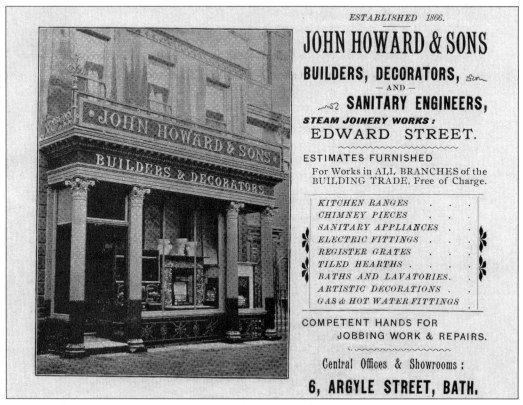

Fig. 118 John Howard & Sons, showrooms in Argyle Street, c.1900. (*BLHS Archives*)

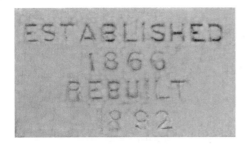

Fig. 119 (*above*) Inscription on the wall of Howard's (former) joinery works in Pulteney Mews. (*BLHS Archives*)

Fig. 120 (*right*) George Russell (1857-1934), a Victorian workman employed by John Howard & Sons. (*Bernard Russell collection*)

Hanks & Whiting, builders and funeral furnishers, later Frederick Hanks & Sons, were in business from about 1904 until 1972. Its founder, Frederick Hanks, was born in Bathwick in 1874 but when he was just three days old his father died leaving his mother with four children to bring up. Frederick, however, was fortunate, being educated at the Bluecoat School, Sawclose, Bath. On leaving school he was apprenticed as a carpenter with John Howard & Sons. In about 1904 he and Ernest Whiting started the business of Hanks & Whiting, builders and funeral furnishers in a stable block in Forester Road. The business grew and by 1920 it employed about 20 plumbers, stonemasons, carpenters and painters. Most of the work involved maintenance on the houses owned by the Bathwick Estate Company but like many builders and carpenters the business was also kept busy with funeral work.

Fig. 121 Hanks & Whiting, Carpenters and Undertakers of Forester Road, c.1900. This building, originally the coach-house for *Beckford Cottage*, is now a private residence. (*Jack and Mary Sparrow collection*)

Fig. 122 Darlington Street, 5th April 1913. The funeral of PC Brimble, furnished by Hanks & Whiting. (*Jack and Mary Sparrow collection*)

In 1920 No.17 Bathwick Street was purchased, the ground floor becoming an office and a nearby piece of their land in Henrietta Gardens accommodating a workshop and mortuary chapel.

Frederick never forgot the struggle his mother had endured in bringing up four children alone and consequently often did work free of charge for anyone he considered needy. Later his sons Douglas and Mervyn joined the business and eventually bought out Frederick's business partner Ernest Whiting. By this time the age of DIY was dawning and although the funeral work continued, fewer men were employed. Frederick Hanks died in 1966 aged 92, his eldest son followed a year later in 1967 aged 57 and Mervyn continued on alone until a bad accident in 1972 forced him to retire and the business finally closed.

Many other small, family-run businesses, established during the Victorian and Edwardian periods, sustained by local customers, survived and continued to serve the parish well into the post-war years.

Villa Fields and The Forester Estate

The 1886 Ordnance Survey map of Bath shows Villa Fields as it was just before its development. This area of Bathwick, bounded by the railway, the river, Bathwick Street and Beckford Road, took its name from *Bathwick Villa*, built in 1777 and demolished in 1897.

Villa Fields remained largely undeveloped until the end of the 19th century: an area of scattered dwellings, orchards and smallholdings, together with the Boating Station buildings, Cleveland Baths and *The Castle Inn*. The roads that were to become Forester Road, Forester Avenue and Forester Lane were already in place, although at that time, unmade and with little or no street lighting.

Fig. 123 A section from the 1886 OS map showing part of Villa Fields. Still visible are the old *Castle Inn*, *Bathwick Villa*, and numerous smaller buildings, together with orchards and gardens. Much of this was demolished to make way for the Forester Estate.

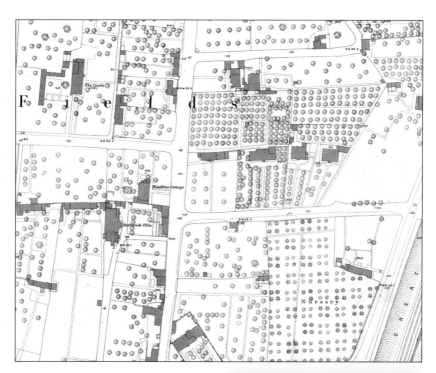

Harry George Vane, 4th and last Duke of Cleveland, died in 1891. By his Will the vast Vane property holdings were broken up and distributed among various heirs. Bathwick and the other Somerset properties passed to his great-nephew, Captain Francis (Frank) Forester (1860-1942) of Darlington, for life. On Frank Forester's death his property was divided between his four children. His widow, Aline, lived at No.103 Sydney Place in Bathwick for a period before her death in 1962. At the time of his inheritance, the Bathwick estate had not been visited by its owners for many years and was badly in need of maintenance and investment. Development of Villa Fields was thus a logical step.

Fig. 124 (*above*) Lord Harry George Vane (1803-1891), 4th (and last) Duke of Cleveland. (*By kind permission of The Lord Barnard TD*)

Fig. 125 (*left*) Captain Francis William Forester (1860-1942). This picture comes from the 1897 Jubilee issue of the *Bath & County Graphic*. After Captain Forester's death at Hurdcott House, Salisbury, in September 1942, his widow, Aline, moved to Sydney Place.

The changes to Villa Fields began with the clearance of three of the four rows of cottages which stood on its western border. The first to go was Villa Place in 1888, followed by Bathwick Place and Cottage Row. Only Kirkham's Buildings was left.[89] These cottages were all accessible from Bathwick Street.

Existing roads were renamed, a few passed out of use and three entirely new ones – Powlett Road, Rockliffe Avenue and Rockliffe Road – were constructed, although the road surface of Rockliffe Avenue (from No.15 onwards) remained unmade until sometime after the end of the 1939-45 war, when it was properly laid as far as the junction with Hampton Row.

The road names are associated with the Forester family, Powlett having been adopted through marriage by some members of the Vane family during the 19th century, and Rockliffe being taken from *Rockliffe Park*, Darlington, a residence of Captain Forester. The former Villa Fields Road became Forester Road around 1900 and the name Powlett Place was changed to the present Forester Avenue. The original name Villa Fields lingered as a part of the postal address for some of the houses in the area until the 1930s. The houses of the Villa Fields area, centred on Forester Road, belong to what is informally known today as the Forester Estate.

Fig. 126 Development in Villa Fields – Forester Road under construction, c.1900. (*Terry Hardick collection*)

These houses, mostly substantial semi-detached villas or modest terrace houses in groups of four, were constructed by various builders (many of whom then retained occupancy) within about 15 years. The smaller terrace houses of Powlett Road (and of what are now Nos.1-4 Forester Avenue[90]) were built of Bristol Cattybrook[91] red brick with some Bath stone detailing, and are still the only brick dwellings in Bathwick.[92] They were the first to be occupied, Nos.1-35 being featured in the 1895 *Bath Post Office Directory*.

Composer and pianist Albert Semprini (1908-1990) of the popular Radio programme, 'Semprini Serenade', was born in Bath and lived at No.20A Powlett Road in 1911. These houses were followed by Nos.1-32 Forester Road, most of Rockliffe Road and Nos.1-8 Rockliffe Avenue before development petered out around 1912. Many of the larger houses were originally given names typical of the time such as *The Lindens* and *Rock Lynn*. Most of the villas, and some of the other houses, once had servants but by the late 1940s these had become the 'daily'.

Fig. 127 John and Emily Stevens outside their home at No.14 Powlett Road in 1924. John Stevens was an assistant brewer at the Bath Brewery (originally called the Bathwick Brewery) on Bathwick Street. Mr and Mrs Stevens were one of the first families to move into Powlett Road where their daughter Mabel was born in 1889. When Mabel died in 1997 in her 108th year (at Stratton on the Fosse) she was reported to be Somerset's oldest lady. (*Christopher Wait collection*)

Fig. 128 Mrs Alice Barter and her daughter Mabel pictured in about 1920 at No.29 Rockliffe Road. The Barter family first lived at No.23 Powlett Road in 1901. In 1906 they moved to Rockliffe Road where they lived for nearly 40 years. Their telephone number was '14'. James Barter was a Police Inspector. He retired from the Police force in 1917 and set up an antiques business in Green Street. (*Bath Record Office, Acc 138*)

Fig. 129 Rockliffe Road, c.1920. This postcard was published by Wm Isaacs, Stationers & Newsagents, No.35 Bathwick Street. The shop was also the post office. William Isaacs was in business there from 1920 to 1930. (*Bath Record Office, Acc 138*)

During this postwar period, from Monday to Friday, it was possible to witness what has been described as 'the march of the brief-case brigade'. Early in the morning Forester Road would be busy as the 'man of the house' (with brief-case) made his way towards the bus stop in Beckford Road, in time to catch the Bathampton bus into the city. The bus arrived and all would board. At almost the same time the bus going in the opposite direction (Bath to Bathampton) would stop, and a small army of 'dailys' would get off and make their way down Forester Road. Later in the day all would be repeated – in reverse!

Various other buildings were constructed on the Forester Estate. The original *Castle Inn*, built 1841, was demolished in 1897 and rebuilt as the public house that stands there today, to a more generous plan using some of the same materials.

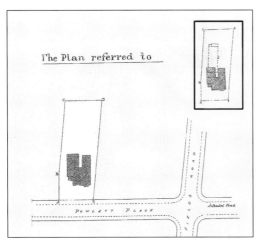

Fig. 130 The rebuilding of *The Castle Inn*. From the 'Agreement Dated 12th January 1897 Bathwick Estate Captain F.W. Forester and Mr George Membery'. The agreement states that the old building should be pulled down and the materials used to build the new one. Note 'Powlett Place', which later became Forester Avenue and Villa Fields Road, which became Forester Road. (*Bath Record Office*) Inset: the old *Castle Inn* superimposed on the plan.

84

Fig. 131 Outside *The Castle Inn*, c.1910. The celebration is unknown. (*David Skelton collection*)

The Parish Rooms for St. John's Church, completed c.1903 in Powlett Road, have had various uses, including a lending library, and now house a picture framing workshop.

In 1939 the fire station was constructed on the edge of the northwest boundary of Villa Fields and the city's fire brigade moved there from Orange Grove. The level of the land that the station stands on was once much lower. In the early 1900s this ground became a rubbish tip. Prior to building, more banking was done and the retaining wall built to curtail the spread of the infill.

The development of Villa Fields as initiated by Captain Forester ceased before the 1914-18 war, 1919 and 1921 seeing attempts to sell his Bathwick holdings. The description of properties listed in the 1919 Bathwick Estate sale catalogue include

> *Villa Fields, including Powlett Road, Forester Road, Rockliffe Road and Forester Avenue. One hundred and eighty attractive Villas together with A fully-licensed public house and A Parish Room the whole producing from Rack Rents and Ground Rent £918 18s. per annum.*

In addition to the above, the sale included the

> *Bath Boating Yard and Boating Station with various outbuildings etc. also nineteen cottages with gardens and uncovered building lands, gardens etc. The whole let on yearly tenancies producing Rack rents £307 0s 4d.*

As well as being the last part of Bathwick developed by a descendant of the Pulteney family, the Forester Estate is especially interesting because of the way it anticipates the transformation of 20th-century Bathwick into a flourishing suburb of Bath.

Fig.132 (*above*) Villa Fields from Cleveland Bridge, c.1919. (*BLHS Archives*)

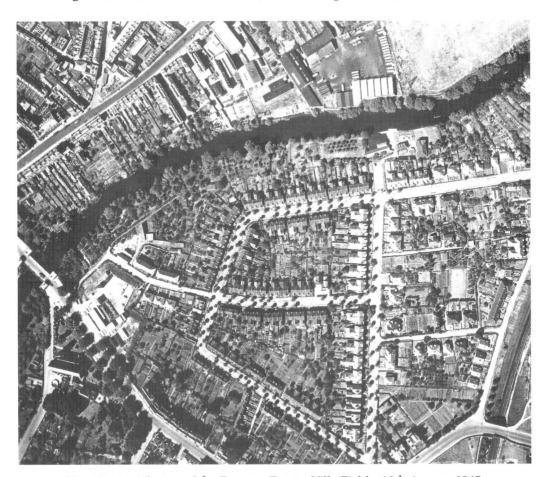

Fig. 133 Aerial view of the Forester Estate, Villa Fields, 10th August 1945.
(*English Heritage, NMR – RAF Photography*)

BUT WHAT WAS THE WEATHER LIKE?

The Years of the Floods

The natural flood plains of Bathwick once stretched along the banks of the River Avon from Ferry Lane on its southern boundary to Grosvenor at the northern end and were often under water. By 1790 the Reverend John Collinson observed that during the winter months the air in Bathwick was damp and foggy and

> *the meads which almost encircle it, frequently underwater by the overflowing of the river from sudden rains ...*[94]

Although by 1809 the increase and severity of the flooding in Bathwick appears to coincide with the Georgian development which had then arrived at the 'road to Claverton' (Bathwick Hill) there are no references to the early floods in the old parish records or any deprivation caused by them.

In 1725 the coldest summer for much of England was recorded when the average temperature reached only 13.1 centigrade (55.5 Fahrenheit). It rained every day from May through to October during which time all low-lying areas suffered almost continuous flooding and the Bath Natural History and Antiquarian Field Club noted

> *that the summer was the most dreadful for continual rains, cold and tempests that ever any history mention, with not a day from May to October without rain ...*[95]

At Monks Mill, just across the river from the Bathwick Mill, an exceptionally high flood was marked. The summer of 1735 was almost as bad and reported to be cold, wet and wintry. In 1774 another flood, equal to the one in 1725, occurred, but neither was as high as in 1809 when a heavy snowfall that lasted several days was followed by a sudden thaw and 'violent' rain. Water poured down the hillsides, rapidly swelling the river and leaving those living near it little time to escape. Distressing scenes are recorded of both human and animal fatalities: wagons, horses, cattle and sheep were swept down river together with the tops of hovels, hayricks and timber.[96] Captain Mainwaring wrote:

> *without doubt, the most agonizing spectacle was that of a cradle floating down the stream, from which an infant now and then endeavoured to raise its head ...*

Fortunately the child was rescued and returned to its distracted parent who lived in the Dolemeads in the neighbouring parish of Lyncombe and Widcombe.

Flooding continued to wreck havoc in the district and in the autumn of 1823, following a very cold and wet July, another massive flood was recorded. Much of Bathwick was again underwater and around the cricket ground and the Dolemeads water lapped the upstairs rooms of dwellings.

By 1824 numerous ideas were being examined by Bath Corporation's newly-established 'Flood Relief Committee' and the great civil engineer Thomas Telford was selected to make a survey. His report stated that

> *it was evident the whole economy of the river banks and channel had been totally changed from its natural state; not with judicious views of perfecting the discharge of flood waters, but for accomplishing 'local objects', these works uniformly creating material obstructions to the course of the waters* [and] *bridges, with inadequate waterways, had been constructed ...*

Telford also referred to buildings and rubbish that had for ages been allowed to encroach and obstruct the river channel and concluded that:

> *while most of the low lands, over which those flood water formerly passed, had been raised by embanked streets, and covered with magnificent buildings (Pulteney-street and its vicinity, Sydney-place, Bathwick Church, &c., for instance); thus confining the said flood waters to the contracted and circuitous channel which now exists ...*

His recommendations included re-shaping and enlarging the river channel downstream from Pulteney Bridge, embanking the low land between the intended Bathwick (Cleveland) Bridge and Pulteney Bridge and improving the direction of the river flow by various engineering operations. The city could not afford the scheme, estimated to cost £47,848 10s and the project was shelved indefinitely. Nothing was done to alleviate any of the problems which were increasing year by year. Meanwhile the weather, as ever, was erratic!

In January 1866 there was severe flooding in all low-lying areas around Bath and Pulteney Road was under water once again. One of the worst floods on record took place on 25th October 1882 when the River Avon rose rapidly the day after prolonged heavy rain.[97] This flood was said to be comparable with that of 1823 but with more casualties, possibly because of the increased population.

Grove Street was badly hit and in places underwater to a depth of several feet. Henrietta Park was also flooded and 18 sheep were drowned while in another part of Bathwick a sow and nine piglets were rescued. Just over the parish boundary, in Widcombe, Police Constable Newton was called to a horse "neighing piteously" in one of the Smallcombe Brewery stables near Princess Buildings, Dolemeads. The Constable, who had already saved several families, gallantly swam to the stable, forced the door and brought out the horse.

Near the *Folly Inn*, a man was reported to be clinging to the top of an apple tree at the back of Cremorne Cottages. The police were alerted to the man's plight and rescued him with boat and rope, apparently no easy task as the water was 20 feet deep and only about 10 to 20 yards from the river bank where the currents were very strong.

The greatest of the Bath floods occurred within a span of three days, from 13th to 15th November 1894. Although overall the water level was some ten inches lower than in 1882, these floods were undoubtedly the most devastating.

The Bath Chronicle reported:

> *The Parish of Bathwick has suffered severely from the visitation and a round of the most affected parts reveal a dismal outlook. Grove Street and St John's Road were deeply inundated. So near did the tide approach Pulteney Street stables that most of the horses had to be removed to a place of safety ...*[98]

The water rose suddenly, flooding the basement kitchens of Henrietta Street and Henrietta Road down to Bathwick Street where cellars and underground kitchens were also under several feet of water. Houses on the river side of St. John's Road were badly affected and had all their vegetables washed away from their gardens. Flood water reached almost as far as the church gates and the local butcher's horse got into difficulties as he tried to pull the cart through the torrent.

The Bath Herald produced a supplement that fully recorded both floods:

the visitation was, indeed, a double one – there were two distinct floods in three days; the first wou'd have been sufficient to have caused an amount of privation and distress about equal to that experienced in the memorable flood of 1882, but the second coming so close upon it and carrying the river so much above the highest level, produced a state of things which is lamentable in the extreme.[99]

The whole of the Avon valley around the city of Bath was studded with huge lakes and low-lying areas cut off from all normal communication. Only the tops of lamp posts were visible across the cricket ground and the Recreation Ground was a vast expanse of water. Henrietta Park was again transformed into a lake, the water spreading in all directions and being as deep in some places as the height of the railings. Villa Fields was another desolate scene and from the railway bridge at Hampton Row a

perfect sea met the gaze and the course of the river could be traced only by the tops of the Pollard trees growing on the banks.

All buildings lying near the river were severely affected and in many cases water reached the upper storeys. The river rose so rapidly that the custodian of the Cleveland Baths and his family barely had time to get out of their house before the water reached the bedroom floors. The water rose to over a foot deep in the bedrooms and completely covered the roof of the dressing rooms that adjoin the house. Fortunately the family were able to shelter in a nearby empty cottage.

As ever the poor and working classes were badly affected and many lost all their possessions. Relief came mainly in the form of handouts via the Flood Relief Committee and clothing and food from the Church. Others were moved to help in practical ways:

The manager of the Bath Brewery Ltd has kindly stated that poor people having wet clothes, bedding, carpets etc can bring them to the Company's houses in Sydney-buildings and the Lower Bristol-road where they can be dried quickly free of charge.

Coal was also ordered and paid for by parish contributions, four tons being distributed to the poor and destitute in Grove Street.

There were more high floods in the 1930s and 1940s but none quite so high or as devastating as that of 1894.

The city experienced two floods in 1960 when Bathwick and Widcombe were badly inundated in October and again at the beginning of December. The December flood was said to be the worst since 1882 and did considerable damage to property. At the boating station one of the main boat-sheds was destroyed but luckily no boats were lost.

The summer of 1968 brought torrential rain and flash flooding again to parts of Bathwick. At this time work began on the long-awaited Flood Prevention Scheme and although held up briefly in 1969 – due to flooding – by 1971 the scheme was finally completed, thereby effectively carrying out the intentions of 1823, 148 years later.

This is not the full story of Bathwick – that has been left for a future generation to discover – but until then why not follow, with R.E.M. Peach[100], the wisdom of Captain Cottle's motto:

When found make a note on't.

Floods in Bathwick
in December 1960.
(*Bath Record Office*)

Fig. 134 (*above*)
Henrietta Road.

Fig. 135 (*right*)
Henrietta Mews.

Fig. 136 (*below*)
Grove Street – almost
all the buildings
on the left are now
demolished except
for St. John's Place
(centre).

Fig. 137 Henrietta Road and Park in December 1960. (*John and Jo Marsh collection*)

Fig. 138 (*above*) The day the Army came to Bathwick. Henrietta Road, July 1968. (*John and Jo Marsh collection*)

Fig. 139 (*right*) Mrs Marsh in her garage at the rear of Henrietta Villas. (*John and Jo Marsh collection*)

The Floods of July 1968.

Fig. 140 (*left*) School is closed! In the lane outside Victoria Infants School, Henrietta Road. (*John and Jo Marsh collection*)

Fig. 141 (*centre*) St. John's Road. (*Neville Field*)

Fig. 142 (*bottom*) Forester Avenue. Note the garages in the centre of the picture where Horton House now stands. (*Neville Field*)

Notes and References

The following abbreviations are used in the notes:

BCL   Bath Central Library
BRO   Bath Record Office
BLHS   Bathwick Local History Society
BRRO Bristol Record Office
SRO   Somerset Record Office
BD   Bath Directories
NMR   English Heritage, National Monuments Record, Swindon
VAG   Victoria Art Gallery

1   *The Countryside Companion*, ed. Tom Stephenson, Odham's Press, London, reprinted 1948.
2   BLHS, *Bathwick: A Forgotten Village*, Millstream Books, Bath, 2004, pp.17-24.
3   Extract from J.E.King, *Somerset Parochial Records, Inventory of Parochial Documents in The Diocese of Bath & Wells and the County of Somerset*, Book 1, Harold King, Taunton, 1938.
4   Glebe Terriers date from 1571-1836. These list church lands and endowments in each parish.
5   John Wroughton, *Stuart Bath: Life in The Forgotten City, 1603-1714*, Lansdown Press, Bath, 2004, p.141. *Somerset Hearth Tax Returns 1664-65*, Public Records Office, London.
6   John Richardson, *The Local Historian's Encyclopaedia*, 2nd edition, Historical Publications, London, 1986, Burial in Wool Acts, 1667 and 1678.
7   Julian Litten, *The English Way of Death: The Common Funeral since 1450*, Robert Hale, London, 1991. Extracts: For a man – 3x3 strokes followed by a stroke for each year of his age; for a woman – 3x2 strokes followed by a stroke for each year of her age; for a child (under 7 years of age) 3x1 stroke and ditto. This custom gradually died out in most of the country except in some local areas, including parts of Somerset where it continued until the onset of World War II in 1939 when all bell-ringing ceased and could only be used as a warning of an impending invasion.
8   *1838 19 December Apportionment of Rent charges in lieu of the Tithes in the Parish of Bathwick between the most noble William Harry Duke of Cleveland, owner of the land and Reverend Peter Gunning, Rector of the said Parish. There is no Common Land.* SRO, ref D/D/rt176.
9   *An Act for Better Paving, Cleansing, Lighting, Watching, Regulating, & Improving, the City of Bath, and the Liberties and Precincts thereof*, 1814. BRO.
10 This appears to have been a small reservoir with a stone surround but the site is unknown. It is mentioned in the *Commissioners Accounts 1815-1846*. BRO.
11 Algernon Capell, Earl of Essex, died in 1709. Under the terms of his will, his son and heir, on reaching his majority in 1726, should settle death duties by disposing of certain estates including that of Bathwick and Wolley (sic). In mediaeval times Woolley belonged, with the estate of Bathwick, to the Nunnery of Wherewell in Hampshire and after Dissolution the ecclesiastical link with Bathwick remained until sometime after 1973.
12 *A Survey of the Manor of Bathwick in the County of Somerset Belonging to the Hon William Pulteney Esq. taken 1727*, British Library. See *Bathwick: A Forgotten Village*, Fig 1.
13 Duty paid to a landowner on the death of a tenant.
14 Extracts from *Copy of a Petition for the Inhabitants of Bathwicke in the County of Somerset*. This document (undated) relates to an Act first passed in the reign of His Majesty King George II. BRRO, ref AC/JS/104(5).
15 William McBryde, Michael Rowe and Gillian Sladen (eds.), *Beyond Mr Pulteney's Bridge*, Bath Preservation Trust, Bath, 1987.
16 Extract from *The Original Bath Guide*, William Lewis, Bath, 1913. "In 1894 the meadows which were formerly Spring Gardens (to which there was a ferry from North Parade) were laid out as the Bath Recreation Ground by a company formed to supply the City with an adequate athletic ground."
17 Council Minutes Vol III, January 1769. "Mr Pulteney to have liberty to build a bridge from Bath to Bathwick at or near the present Ferry, the Corporation allow a way thereto from High

Street provided he buys at his own expense from the present possessors such houses and lanes as interfere with the said way and are not in poss. of the Corporation. On execution that the Articles signed by Mr Pulteney in 1768 24 Dec be complied with and that the Corporation may have liberty to insert a Clause as they shall think fit." BRO.

18 R.S. Neale, *Bath, A Social History 1680-1850*, Routledge & Kegan Paul, London, 1981, p.38.

19 Two leases dated and granted 1st April 1788, between Henrietta Laura Pulteney, George Clark and William Phillips and also between W. Pulteney, Miss Pulteney and Wm. Mathews, mealman. BRO.

20 Contract between Henrietta Laura Pulteney and William Upsell, 10 February 1792. SRO, ref DD/BR/tjf 3.

21 Richard T.A. Irving, *A History of the Byfield Mine, Combe Down*, Combe Down Heritage Society, Bath, 2005.

22 John Pinch 1769-1827, born Callington, Cornwall, son of a carpenter.

23 *Bathwick Vestry Minutes Book 1791-1805*. SRO, ref. D/P/batw.m.9/1/1.

24 A 'Workhouse' was included in the Act of 1815 for the Bathwick New Church and is believed to have been built in Little Grove Street. On Cotterell's map of Bath 1852, this appears to have been a small lane that ran towards the river next to where Caxton Court now stands. Caxton Court was redeveloped in 1982 from the 19th-century malthouse and brewhouse belonging to the Northgate Brewery which previously occupied that site. The Union Workhouse was built to take the poor from 24 parishes in and around Bath and that building later became part of St. Martin's Hospital.

25 *Bathwick Vestry Minutes Book 1791-1805*. SRO, ref. D/P/batw.m.9/1/1.

26 Letter dated 25th July 1802, reference as above.

27 Mrs Bolwell was reported to be the first inhabitant of Great Pulteney Street, where for many years she kept a lodging house. At the age of 23 she was made a member of the Methodist Society by the Reverend John Wesley when he set up his first preaching room in Avon Street, Bath. She died in Bathwick in 1829 aged 83.

28 *Waywardens Accounts 1802. James Goodridge and John Starr*. SRO, ref. D/P/batw.m14/5/1.

29 Thomas Townsend (1733-1800), 1st Viscount Sydney, supported the establishment of a penal colony at Botany Bay and appointed Admiral Phillips to govern the settlement which in 1788 was named Sydney in honour of Townsend. In 1793 Admiral Phillips retired to Bath and Sydney Place was named after his friend the Viscount. The link with Pulteney is obscure but is possibly through Parliamentary or Government connections.

30 Lease dated: *26 day of March 1792, Henrietta Laura Pulteney, Charles Lewis and Thomas Baldwin*. BRO.

31 *Bathwick Vestry Minutes Book 1791-1805*. SRO, ref. D/P/batw.m.9/1/1.

32 *The Bath Weekly Chronicle & Herald, Notes & Queries*, 1940-1944. BCL.

33 Henrietta Laura Pulteney died in 1808 aged 42 years. William Henry (known as Harry) Vane, also born in 1766, was thus the same age when he inherited the Estate of Bathwick. Lord Vane later succeeded to the Dukedom of Cleveland.

34 *Beyond Mr Pulteney's Bridge*.

35 William Henry (Harry) Vane was succeeded in turn by his three brothers. All four were consecutive Dukes of Cleveland, the Dukedom being revived in 1833.

36 *The Bath Journal*, 15th January 1810.

37 The waterway at Bathwick and the wharves are covered in *Bathwick: A Forgotten Village*, pp. 50-65.

38 Pierce Egan, *Walks through Bath*, Meyler, Bath, 1819. There was great relief when Napoleon abdicated in 1814. BCL.

39 *Act to Build a New Church & Workhouse in the Parish of Bathwick*, 1815. A quarter of an acre of ground in Grove Street was purchased for ten shillings and a workhouse appears to have been built, see ref. 24 above. Diocese of Bath & Wells.

40 Richard Mann, *Historical Sketches of Bath Churches*, Mitchell, Plymouth, 1912, p.93.

41 *The Bath Chronicle*, 1817.

42 Rowland Mainwaring, *Annals of Bath 1800-1835*, Meyler, Bath 1838.

43 R.E.M. Peach, *Historic Houses in Bath and their Associations*, Simpkin Marshall, London & R.E.M. Peach, Bath, 1898.

44 This ancient word first referred to cages for keeping hawks in at the rear of a property when moulting or 'mewing'. In 1534 King Henry had his stables built on his estates where the mews had been.

45   *Bathwick: A Forgotten Village*, p.13. In 1809 the watch box was removed from Laura Place and the site was later grassed over. There are numerous entries in the records for 'mowing grass in Laura Place' in *Bathwick Commissioners Accounts 1815-1856*. BRO.

46   R.E.M. Peach, *Street Lore of Bath*, Simpkin Marshall, London & E.R. Blackett, Bath, 1893.

47   *The Bath Chronicle Weekly*, 10th January 1833.

48   Lawrence H. Officer and Samuel H. Williamson, *Five Ways to Compute the Relative Value of a UK Pound Amount 1830 to Present*, MeasuringWorth.com, 2007.

49   Gerrard's Buildings were designed by the Bath Architect, Molly Gerrard and named after her husband, Major Ronald Gerrard, killed in enemy action in North Africa in 1943. In 1937, as Molly Taylor, Mrs Gerrard designed *Kilowatt House*, North Road. This building is one of the 20th-century houses that stand on the site of the old Bathwick quarries.

50   Henry Edmund Goodridge designed Beckford's Tower, Lansdown (1825) and many of the Italianate villas on Bathwick Hill. He later succeeded John Pinch (died 1827) as Lord Darlington's architect to the Bathwick estate.

51   *Deed of Settlement, The Right Hon William Harry, Earl of Darlington and The Bathwick Bridge Company, 24 May 1826*. BRO.

52   The contractor was John Vaughan who at the time was also working on the construction of Beckford's Tower at Lansdown. This information is also verified by a rough handwritten order and receipt for brass pipes for the tower that was sent to him 'c/o Toll House, The Bridge' in 1827. These papers were found at Trowbridge Record Office by Dr Pat Hughes while she was working on Beckford research in about 1999. For John Vaughan – see *Bathwick: A Forgotten Village*, pp.53-55.

53   *The Bath & Cheltenham Gazette*, 25th December 1838.

54   Extract from S.D. Major, *Notabilia of Bath*, London, 1871.

55   George Stothert, one of the opponents, was already producing coal gas for use in his foundry – forerunner of Stothert and Pitt.

56   Dr Wilkinson lived in Bathwick in later life and his gravestone (giving his middle name as 'Hannings') can be seen close to Bathwick Street in St Mary's Old Churchyard.

57   *Eastwick's Journal at Bath Gas Station 1819-1820*, Museum of Bath at Work.

58   *The Bath Chronicle*, 21st May 1829.

59   *The Bath Chronicle*, 11th June 1829.

60   Minutes of Trustees for building a new church, 1825-1840. SRO.

61   Hugh Torrens, *The Evolution of a Family Firm: Stothert and Pitt of Bath*, Bath, 1978.

62   Church Land for the use of the incumbent Rector. See Note 4.

63   *The Bath Chronicle Weekly*, 10th May 1855.

64   *Indenture Deed & Plan, June 13 1858 between Lord Powlett and Trustees, Burial Board of Bathwick*. BRO.

65   *The Bath Chronicle Weekly*, 24th January 1861.

66   These graves were maintained by church members under the terms of a private fund then administered by the church.

67   The exceptions being where there is space in family plots previously purchased and where space permits the internment of ashes.

68   St. John's Church vestry papers.

69   'The beginnings of St. John Baptist, Bath', a handwritten document initialled E.I.B., St John's Church vestry papers.

70   Balance sheet 26th January 1872, St John's vestry papers.

71   *The Bath Chronicle Weekly*, 1st November 1838. The school is now a private residence and having fallen out of use as an educational establishment the land has reverted to the Vane family.

72   *Bathwick Parochial School: Managers and Subscribers Minutes Book 1887-1903*. (Access No.102, addnl.) BRO.

73   Collection of Records, Minutes Books and Papers relating to Victoria Infants and Bathwick Parochial School from 1838-1903, as above. BRO.

74   The Reverend Francis Kilvert and his brother John, a surgeon, were the uncles of the Reverend Francis Kilvert the diarist. Rev. Francis Kilvert often preached at St. Mary's Church and occasionally conducted funeral services in the parish. John Kilvert was resident for over 50

years in Bathwick at No.12 Darlington Street and was highly regarded both as a skilled surgeon and a benevolent Christian man who tended the poor and destitute.

75   This building now houses The Holburne Museum of Art.

76   No.4 Darlington Street was previously a school in 1910. It was also once the residence of Euclid Shaw, barge owner; see *Bathwick: A Forgotten Village*, pp.51-53.

77   *A Map of the Manor of Bathwick in the County of Somerset drawn for William Pulteney Esq.* (c.1770). The site was also confirmed by transposing the relevant section of the early maps onto the 1886 OS map at the same scale. BRO.

78   *The Bath Journal*, 9th February 1786.

79   It is probable that the 'free ferry' not only served both Bathwick and the Grosvenor Pleasure Gardens but also provided a means of getting to the turnpike road.

80   *Counterpart Agreement for Ground for Building between His Grace the Duke of Cleveland and Mr Matthew William Jones Hulbert. 10th June 1839 ... Surveyed by John Pinch* [the younger]. BRO.

81   The original 'Cremorne Pleasure Gardens' were situated on the banks of the River Thames at Chelsea Farm, London, and were named after Viscount and Lady Cremorne who owned that Estate.

82   Complaint from Miss Barlow of Cleveland Villa, entry dated 3rd June 1865, *Bath Watch Committee Minutes Book*. Counter complaint, dated 9th June 1865, from Mr Osmond regarding people bathing in the canal near his premises is also entered in the *Minutes*. BRO.

83   In 1919 Captain Forester put the Bathwick Estate up for sale but it did not sell and was subsequently withdrawn. The Estate was put up for auction again in 1921 (with various properties excluded) and this time most of the lots were sold off, many to the leaseholders and occupiers. The Bathwick Estate Company was formed in 1924 to maintain its existing properties and continued to do so until 1973 when 56 Georgian houses and other buildings were purchased by Bath City Council. Later Smallcombe Farm was bought by The National Trust and building land and various ground rents were also sold off. The Company was then wound up by the Trustees.

84   *Bathwick: A Forgotten Village*, Fig. 1.

85   *The Bath Chronicle*, 24th June 1897.

86   As above

87   The Jubilee Oak is still there today and has since been joined by the Coronation Oak, planted across the park to the northwest to commemorate the crowning of Queen Elizabeth II in June 1953.

88   *Boodle Collection*, Vol.18, p.63. BCL.

89   *Bathwick: A Forgotten Village*, pp.36-42.

90   These houses appear as Nos.1-4 Powlett Place in the 1898 *Post Office Directory* but as Nos.1-4 Rockliffe Avenue (their addresses today) in the 1900 *Directory*. More houses followed: *Dated 16th January 1899, Bathwick Estate Capt. F.W. Forester and Mr George Membery, Duplicate Agreement for a lease of land in Powlett Place for Building*. This lease was for four houses – Nos.21-24 Powlett Place, later called Forester Avenue. The builder was Mr Erwood. BRO.

91   The Cattybrook Brick Works near Bristol, started by Charles Richardson in 1864, provided engineering (good) quality bricks for numerous other local projects, including lining the Severn Tunnel and the chocolate factory at Keynsham.

92   The Bath Corporation Act of 1925 gave the city the power 'to make bye-laws as to the material and construction of buildings' and the current formal requirement for Bath stone construction in the city stems from this. BRO.

93   Rockliffe Avenue was renumbered in the 1930s, and these eight houses became the odd-numbered 1-15, as they are today.

94   The Reverend John Collinson, *The History and Antiquities of the County of Somerset*, Cruttwell, Bath, 1791, p.9. See also *Bathwick: A Forgotten Village*, p.14.

95   Barry Horton, *West Country Weather Book*, Barry Horton, Bristol, 1995.

96   *Annals of Bath, 1800-1835*, p.82.

97   *The Bath Herald*, October 1882.

98   *The Bath Chronicle Weekly*, 15th November 1894.

99   *A Record of The Great Floods in Bath and the Surrounding District, November 13 & 15th 1894*, reprinted from *The Bath Herald*, printed at the Bath Herald Office, North Gate Street, Bath, 1894.

100   *Street Lore of Bath.*

Appendix

Bathwick street names associated with the Pulteney family or their successors:

Alva Street (not built)	William Johnstone Pulteney. Johnstone family of Alva, Scotland.
Great Annandale Street (not built)	William Johnstone Pulteney. Connection with the Marquis of Annandale, Scotland.
Argyle Buildings/Street	political connection with Duke of Argyle.
Barnard Villas	Baron Barnard of Raby.
Cleveland Bridge/Walk	Duke of Cleveland.
Daniel Street	Daniel Pulteney, grandfather of Henrietta Laura Pulteney.
Darlington Place/Road	Earl of Darlington.
Dunsford Place	unknown connection.
Edward Street	Edward Vane of Raby.
Forester Road/Avenue	Captain Francis William Forester.
Frances Square (not built)	Frances Pulteney (mother of Henrietta Laura) inherited estate in 1767.
Grove Street	unknown connection.
Henrietta Street/Road	Henrietta Laura Pulteney.
Henry Street (not built)	Henry Vane.
Heydon Street (not built)	intended as 'Heddon'. William Pulteney's (Earl of Bath) Parliamentary seat in Yorkshire.
Johnstone Street	William Johnstone Pulteney.
Laura Place	Henrietta Laura Pulteney.
Powlett Road	Sophia Powlett (Paulett), wife of Henry Vane.
Pulteney Street/Road	family name.
Raby Place	Raby Castle, Darlington.
Rockliffe Avenue/Road	Captain Forester's estate at Darlington.
Sackville Street (not built)	William Pulteney (Earl of Bath) owned Sackville Street, London.
Stanhope Street (not built)	political connection with Lord Stanhope.
Sunderland Street	Earl of Sunderland connection with Margaret Tichborne, wife of Daniel Pulteney, grandmother of Henrietta Laura.
Sutton Street	Sir Richard Sutton and Eliz. Evelyn Sutton, connection with Henrietta Laura's grandmother – Margaret Tichborne.
Sydney Buildings/Place	Thomas Townsend, 1st Viscount Sydney. Parliamentary connection.
Tourville Street (not built)	Probably named after the French aristocratic family, who after their escape to this country during the French Revolution, were amongst those who were helped by William Johnstone and Henrietta Laura Pulteney.
Upper Great Pulteney Street (not built)	family name.
Vane Street	Vane family.
William Street	William Johnstone Pulteney.

INDEX

This index covers the two volumes, *Bathwick: A Forgotten Village* and *Bathwick: Echoes of the Past*. References to the first volume are given first, prefixed by the letter 'f'; those to the second volume are prefixd by the letter 'e'. References to illustrations are given in bold.

Allen John f30
Allen, Ralph f55, 78, 81; e17, 18
Allen, Ralph Shuttleworth e18
Alma Tavern f58; e42
Alva Street f47
Ambrose, Ambrose f65
Amery, F.J. & Sons e68
Andrews, Colonel Augustus e71
Angell's Furniture Repository f56
Argyle Chapel e56
Argyle Court f85
Argyle Mill f79
Argyle Street (Argyle Buildings) f79, **80**, 84, 85;
    e16, **33**, 73, 76, 78
Argyle Tavern e78
Asquith, Herbert and Cynthia e51, **51**
Atwood, Thomas Warr f81
Aust, James e66
Austen, Jane e**23**

Back, Silas and family f66
Bagshaw, John e24
Bailey, Samuel Inkerman f70, 71, **71**
Baird, Hugh, & Sons f58
Baldwin, Thomas e16, 19, 23, 24
Bargeman's Tavern, The f58
Barker, Benjamin e30, **31**
Barley [Mow], The e78
Barnard Villas e39
Barry's Court f85
Barter, Alice, James and Mabel e**83**
Batchelor, Thomas e8
Bath Carriage Works e36, **36**
Bath Cats and Dogs Home e76
Bath City Police Force f82
Bath College for Boys e71
Bath Corporation Pleasure Grounds C'tee e72-3
Bath Dolphins f72
Bath Gas Light and Coke Company e44
Bath Humane Society f63, **64**
Bath Lido f72
Bath Mineral Water Hospital e50
Bath (Proprietary) College e61, **61**, 72
Bath Rugby Club e78
Bath Spa Hotel e**70**, 71, **71**
Bath Volunteer Regiment/(Rifle) Corps f47; e28
Bathampton f10, 39, 40; e7, 18, 19, **19**, 37, 43, 84

Bathwick (Bath) Brewery f11, 36, **37**, **41**; e78, 83, 89
Bathwick Bridge Company e38
Bathwick Carriage Works f56, 57
Bathwick Commissioners e44-46
Bathwick Down e17
Bathwick Estate Company f41; e67, 78, 79
Bathwick Farm f31, 32, **32**
Bathwick Grange e46
Bathwick Hill f6, 21, 49, 51, **57**;
    e28, 29, 35, 39, 43, 46, 47, 51, 61, **77**, 87
Bathwick Hill Stores e77
Bathwick House f33-35, **33**, **34**, **35**
Bathwick Lane e13
Bathwick Manor e7-11, 12-14, **12**, 62, 66
Bathwick Meadows f15, 46, 77-79; e14, 16
Bathwick Mews e34-36, **34**
Bathwick Mill f79-80, **79**, **80**; e**15**, 72, 87
Bathwick Mortuary Chapel f23-30, **23-30**
Bathwick Nurseries f67
Bathwick Park e72
Bathwick Place f39, 41; e82
Bathwick Police Act e44, 47
Bathwick Pound f16, **16**
Bathwick Quarries e17-20, **18**, **20**
Bathwick Rugby Football Club e**75**
Bathwick St Mary's Junior School f63, 67
Bathwick Schools f78, 86; e56-61, **57-61**, 67
Bathwick Street f10, 11, 20, 21, 22, 33, 34, **35**, 36,
    38, 41, 77;
    e19, **26**, **27**, 37, 48, 52, 58, 72, 76, 78, 80, 83, 88
Bathwick Tavern, The f58
Bathwick Terrace e29
Bathwick Villa f43-48, **43-46**, **48**, 77; e14, **81**
Bathwick Wood f10, **10**; e15
Bear Inn, The e76
Beckford Cottage e**79**
Beckford Gardens f75; e43
Beckford Road f44, 67; e80, 84
Beckford's Tower f53
Beefsteak Tavern, The e60
Biggs, Ann f13
Biggs, Mr e58
Blomfield, Arthur e55
Blount, Charles f30, **30**
Blow's Coffee House f85
Bluecoat School f16; e79
Board of Commissioners and Watch C'tee e11

Boater, The e78
Boating Station e65-67, **65-66**, 80, 85
Boatstall Lane and Meadows f11, 15; e16, **16**
Bodywork Ltd. e**69**
Bolwell, Flower f11, 19; e23
Bottled Ale & Porter Stores, The f84
Bourne, Austin and Newport, Messrs f69, 70
Bourne, William f70
Bowler, Jonathan Burdett f41
Brabazon, Anthony Beaufort e50, **50**
Brimble, PC William f**76**; e**80**
Brisbane, Dame Eleanora f28
Bristow, Nimrod f41
Brompton House f20, **28**, **31**
Brooks, Samuel f58; e42
Brown, John f75
Browne & Gill f**41**
Brymer, James e49
Buck, Samuel and Nathaniel e**13**
Burney, Fanny f45, 46

Camden Crescent e62
Canal House f55
Cantle, W.H. f56, **56**
Caroline Buildings f64
Carpenter, Robert f51
Carriage Road f78
Case, John f44
Castle [Inn], The e78, 80, **81**, 84, **84**, **85**
Castle Lane e46
Castle Tavern, The (*Castle Villa*) e**64**, 70, **70**
Castle View f56, 60, **60**, **61**
cemeteries, *see* Smallcombe Vale Cemeteries
Chant, Philip e**59**
Chappell, John f58
Charlotte Dundas f61
Charmbury family f54, 55
Cheapside f85
Church Street f52; e47
Churchill, Winston e71
Clark, George f**4**, 16; e16
Clark, W. Tierney e**40**
Clarke, Robert f51
Claverton f11, 12, 16, 49, 51; e12, 13, **13**, **19**, 28, 39
Claverton Lodge e51, 61, **61**
Cleveland Arms, The and Brewery f53, 56, **56**, 58, **58**, 59, **59**
Cleveland Baths f66, 69-72, **69**, **71-72**, 73; e80, 89
Cleveland Bridge f6, 15, **15**, 20, 53, 77; e35, 37-38, **37-38**, 42, 66, 67, 88
Cleveland Cottages f15
Cleveland, Duke of f32, 41, 45, 55, 69, 78; e18, 28, **28**, 29, 48, 57, 63, 81
Cleveland House f55
Cleveland Row f70, 74-76, **74**, **75**, **76**

Cleveland Tavern, The f75
Cleveland Walk f9, 49; e39
Clevelands, The f58, 59
Coalbrookdale Ironworks f51
Coard, Peter f42
Cold Water Baths f64-66, **65**, **66**
Coles e45
Collins, A. f16
Collinson, Reverend John f12, 14, 31, 77; e87
Comper, Sir Ninian e**55**
Cottage Row f38, **38**, 39, 41; e82
Cotterell, mapmaker e44
Countess of Huntingdon's Chapel f44, **44**
Cremorne Cottages e88
Cremorne Gardens e62-65, **64**
Crown Inn, The f11, 18, 19, 41, 64; e**76**, 78

Daniel Street f8; e24, 25, **26**, **27**, 46, 75, 78
Darlington, Earl of f21; e24, 28, **28**, 29, 30, 37
Darlington Farm f69
Darlington Mews e34
Darlington Road f67; e**59**, 60
Darlington Street f29, 53; e50, 61, 80
Darlington Villa e60
Darlington Wharf f50, 62-64, **62-64**, 66, 69, 70; e43
Day & English e78
Defence of the Country Act e27
Denny, Lady Charlotte e32
Dolemead(s) f78; e62, 87, 88
Doshi, Mr. B. e**33**
Drought, Frances e60
Duke of Cambridge, The f84
Dunn, Reverend James f31; e56, **56**
Dyer, William f30

Edward Street e51, 78
Emery & Sons f69
Ennix, The f34, 43; e65
Essex, Earl of e12
Evans, W. f**70**
Eveleigh, John f83, 84; e26
Evill, M. f16
Evill, Sam e30
Ewens, William e35

Falconor, Mr f79
Falkeners or Falkners Mills f79; e22
Fern Bank e67
ferries f14, **14**, 15, **15**, 16, 77; e66
Ferry Lane f15, 16; e87
Ferry, James f43-46
Ferry, Peter f43, **44**
Fireman's Arms, The f84
Fisher, Abel f19
Fisher, Fred e66-67, **66**

Fisher, George e73
Fisherman's House f75
floods e87-92, **90-92**
Folly, The e62-65, **62**, **63**, 88
Folwell, Miss e**59**
Forester, Aline e81
Forester Avenue f33; e78, 80, 82, 85
Forester Estate f43, 48; e80-86, **81**, **84**, **86**
Forester Lane e80
Forester Road f44, 48; e79, **79**, 80, 82-85, **84**, **92**
Forester, Captain Francis William f41;
    e51, 72, 73, 76, 81, **81**, 82, 84, 85
Fosbery, George Vincent, VC e51, **51**
Frances Square e24, 72
Frances Street e24
Francis e45
Fuller, Thomas e49

Gallaways Buildings f43
Garlands Coach Manufactory f84
Geoffrey, Bishop of Coutances f8
George's House f**57**, **62**
George's Place f8, **62**; e76, **77**
Gerrard's Buildings e36
Gerrish, Peter e**22**
Gibbs, Thomas W. f74
Giles, Charles Edward e54
Gill, John Elkington f74
Gillard, Walter and family f67-69, **68**
Gilpen, Sir Joseph f29
Glover, John e28
Goddard, James f79
Godfrey, Reverend Race f70
Godwin, H. e**25**
Gollege's sweet shop f75
Goodden, Wyndam f25
Goodridge, Alfred Samuel e50, **52**
Goodridge, Henry Edmund f55; e37, 46
Goodridge, James f**4**, 55; e24, 46
Goodridge, James Frederic e46
Grapevine Cottage f66, 67
Gravel Walk f78
Great Pulteney Street f6, 13, 32, 39, 40, 47; e16,
    24, **24**, 25, 28, 33, 35, **35**, 39, 61, **61**, 72, 73, 88
Great Western Railway f8, 55, 56, 63, 64, 66;
    e29, 2-44, **43-44**, 47, 63, 70
Green, Charles e45
Greenway Lane e76
Gregory, George f71, 85
Grigg, Reverend Peter f13, 31
Grimm, Samuel I. e**17**
Grosvenor e62, 87
Grosvenor Bridge f10, 11; e44, **44**, 63
Grove Street f77-86, **77**, **80-83**, **85-86**;
    e20, **21**, 34, 35, 56, 67, 68, 78, 88, 89, **90**

Guest, Thomas f16
Guildhall e33, **33**
Gunning, Peter e29

Haigh, Emily e76
Hale, Henry e58
Hamilton, Reverend Leveson Russell e53, 54
Hampton Museum, The f75; e49
Hampton Row f53, 63, 66, 69, 73-76, **73**, **76**;
    e43, **43**, 49, 63, 82, 89
Hampton Way e62
Hanks & Whiting f76; e79, **79**, **80**
Hanks, Frederick and family e79-80
Hantone f10
Harbutt, Noel f79, **80**
Harcourt Masters, Charles e62
Hardick, Dan e65
Hardick, Rosetta e**67**
Harris, Walter f24; e29, 30
Hat and Feather yard f8
Hawkins, Eli Cornelius and family f56, 58, 59
Heath, Reverend William e8
Henrietta Buildings f85; e87
Henrietta Court f45
Henrietta Gardens f8; e76, 80
Henrietta Mews e34, **90**
Henrietta Park f8, 11, 78;
    e25, 61, 72-75, **73-75**, 76, 88, 89, **91**
Henrietta Place f85
Henrietta Road f23, 30, 77, 78;
    e24, 39, 42, 48, 88, **90-92**
Henrietta Street f24, 78; e16,22, 37, 42, 46, 54, 88
Henrietta Villas e**42**, **68**, **91**
Herbert, Captain f30
Hill, John e**21**
Hobson, E. f22, **22**
Hobson, George f**43**, 44
Hobson, Henry f**21**
Holly Cottage f48
'Home for Strays' e75-76, **75**
Hooper, Francis f58, 59, 66
Horsell, William f64, **65**
Horton House f15; e**92**
Howard, John, & Sons e78, **78**, 79, **79**
Hulance, William f38, 41; e19
Hulbert, William and family e63, **63**, **64**
Huson, Reverend Richard e8-9

Jefferis Cottage f67
Jefferis, Samuel and family f67-69
Jehovah's Witnesses f72
Johnstone Street e16, 44, 45
Jones, Charles Gee f28
Jones, John e**34**
Jones, Richard f81

Judd, Thomas f16

Kelson, Susanna e47
Kemble, Reverend Charles e71
Kennet & Avon Canal f23, 37, 50, 51, 55, **61**, 63, 64,
    74; e**19**, 29, **29**, 42-43, **43**, 70, 78
Kilvert, Reverend Francis and Leonora e61
Kilvert, John e50
King and Tuck e46
King Edward's School f10
Kingsmead Terrace e45
Kirkham, Samuel and family f**4**, 36, 37, 39-40, **40**,
    41, 42
Kirkham's Buildings f9, **9**, 36-42, **36-39**, **41-42**; e82

La Sainte Union Convent School e60
La Touche, Ellen f30, **30**
Ladies Seminary and Boarding School e60, **60**
Lamb, The f75
Lansdown, Joseph f52, **52**, 56; e11, 49
Large, John f65
Laura Chapel f24
Laura Place f13, **13**; e16, **17**, 33, 35, **35**, 44
Lawrence, Mary e**32**
Lear Lane f12
Lever, Harry Edgar f59
Lewis, William e8
Lockey, Reverend Francis e**40**
Lockyer, John e**13**
London Road e37
Longstrat, Mr e25
Lowther, Caroline f45, **45**
Lyncombe, *see* Widcombe

Mackinnon, John f18
Mainwaring, Captain Rowland f51; e33, 87
Malthouse, The f58
Maltsters, The (Baird & Sons) e78
Mann, George Charmbury f74; e42, 49, 54, 55
Mann's School for Girls e56
Marks, Matthew Henry e70
Marks, William Henry e70
Marrett, Wine Merchant f46
Marsh, Jo e**91**
Marshall, Charles e**20**
Marshman, John e67, 68
Maslen, Benjamin e**32**
Mathews, William e16
Maynard, Charles e66
Maynard, Ernest e66
Membery, George e84
Mills & Sons f62
Milsom Street e**33**
Minerva Court e**69**
Ministry of Defence f69

Minster Way f69
Monks Mill f**79**; e**14**, 87
Montebello e46
Moorings, The f56, 57
Mrs Bedford's Motor Car Works e36, **36**

Narrow Lane f67, **67**
Nattes, J.C. e**21**
Neville family e12
New Sydney Place e24, 30, 32-33, 60, **60**
Newton, Police Constable e88
Newtown e23, 38
Noel, Sir Gerrard e32
North Parade f43; e39
North Parade Bridge f15; e39, **40-41**
North Road f10, **10**; e17, 18, **18**, **39**, 61
North Road Lodge e**39**
Northgate Brewery f84
Norwood Farm f8

"Old Bill' f75
Orange Grove f82; e85
Osmond, Thomas e63-64, **64**
Ostrich Court f85
Ostrich Tavern, The f84

Packet Station f63, **64**
Palmer, Daniel e**9**
Palmer, James f31, 78
Palmer, John f19
Palmer, William f16
Parochial Junior School f78, 86; e56-60, **58-59**
Parsonage House f31, **31**, **32**
Paxton, Mr e45
Peach, R.E.M. e89
Peacock family f51, 52
Peacock's Wharf f52, **52**, 56, 58, **61**
Pearce, Richard e62
Penny, P.E. e**77**
Pert's Dye Works e73
Philips (Phillips), William f16; e16
Phipps, Joseph and Louisa f59
Pickwick, Moses f16; e35
Pike, John Henry and family f82
Pile Corner f11; e44, **44**
Pinch, Charles f27
Pinch, John the elder f23, 24, 27, 34, 47, 52, 55, 58, 73;
    e19, **20**, 22, 24, 25, 29, **29**
Pinch, John the younger f27, 53, 54, **54**, 55, 78;
    e58, **63**
Pinch (*née* Cheave), Martha f27; e**20**
Pinch, William f45, 58
Pinchin Sims & Co. f58
Pinch's Folly f45, **45**
Pine Coffin, Colonel e44

Police Office f62
Pollinger, A.E. e36
Poole, Samuel e**62**
Powell, Miss e55
Powlett Court f36, 42
Powlett Place e82, 84
Powlett Road f9, **9**, 33, 34, 36; e82, **83**, 85
Powlett, Lord f45, **45**; e18, 54
Prentice, Reverend Richard e47
Prior, A. f16
Priory Lodge e47
Prison, Bath City f81-82, **81**, **82**, **83**; e14
Pritchard, Mr f78
Public Baths, Old Darlington Wharf f66
Pulteney (Pulteney's) Arms, The f28; e24, 25, 28
Pulteney Bridge f6, 11, 15, 16, 81;
    e14, **14**, **15**, 16, **17**, 22, 33, 37, **40**, 49, 88
Pulteney, Daniel e14, 24
Pulteney, Frances e14, 16, 24
Pulteney, Harry e14
Pulteney, Henrietta Laura f38; e16, 20, 24, 28
Pulteney Mews e34, 35, 36, **36**, 78, **79**
Pulteney Road e60, 88
Pulteney, William f6, 10, 11, 21, 31, 34, 37, 47, 63,
    77, 78, 81; e6, 12-14, 17, 22, 23, 28, 37, 65
Pulteney, William Johnstone f6; e14, 16
Pursey, Mr e**59**

Quarry Road e18
Queen Charlotte e32-33, **33**
Queen Victoria, The f75, **76**

Raby Place f52, 53, 56, **57**; e29, 33, 47
Raby Villa f53, 54, **54**, 55
Raby Villas f**60**
Radnedge family f69
Recreation Ground f78; e14, 89
Rendezvous Club f59
Rennie, John f63; e42
Richardson, Alfred f56
Richardson's Garage f**57**
Rifleman's Arms, The e**27**
Rising Sun, The (Rising Sun & Lark) f84, 86; e78
Robins, Thomas f11, **12**, 17, 31, 33, 34, **34**
Robinson, William f51, 53, 55, **56**
Rochfort Place f34
Rockliffe Avenue e43, 82, 83
Rockliffe Park, Darlington e82
Rockliffe Road e82
Rosenburg, Charles f**22**
Rosery, The e67-68, **68**
Royal Crescent e32
Royal Oak, The f84
Rudhall, I. f25
Russell, George e**79**

St. James Parish e22
St. John the Baptist Church f9-10, 11, 20, **20**, 22,
    22, 31, 74;
    e42, 52-56, **54-55**, 67, **67**, 85
St. John's Place f**85**; e**90**
St. John's Road f77; e58, 60, 67-69, **67-69**, 70, 88, **92**
St. Lawrence (old) Bridge f16, 78
St. Mary intra Muros Church f81
St. Mary the Virgin New Church f6, 21, 24, **24**,
    26, **26**, 55, 62;
    e29-32, **29**, **31**, **32**, 35, 46-47, **47**, 50, 52-53
St. Mary the Virgin Churchyard, Smallcombe Vale
    see Smallcombe Vale Cemeteries
St. Mary's Old Church (Bathwick Parish Church)
    f17-22, **17-22**, 26, **26**, 47; e7, **9**, 24
St. Michael's, Walcot f24
St. Nicholas School e61, **61**
Sam's Court f39, 41
Saxty, John f13
Scarth, Reverend H.M. and family f27; e49, 50
Selassie, Haile e71
Semprini, Albert e83
Sham Castle f10; e18
Sham Castle Lane f8; e70-71, **70**
Shaw, Euclid e29, 51, 52, 53, **53**
Silk, Mr e**33**
Smallcombe Mortuary Chapel f74; e42, **48**
Smallcombe Vale e17, 51
Smallcombe Vale Cemeteries f55;
    e42, 48-52, **48-53**, 54, 78
Smallcombe Wood e16, 49
Smith, John f58
Smith, Thomas f16
South Parade f15
South West Gas Company f59
Spring Gardens f6, 15, 47, 77, 78, **80**, 86;
    e14, **15**, 16, 72, 78
Spring Gardens Lodge f79, **80**
Stevens, Emily, John and Mabel e**83**
Stockham, William and family f59, **59**
Stothert and Pitt f65; e47
Stothert, George f51, 52; e47
Stothert, John and family e45, **45**, 46-47, **46**
Strange, John e36, **36**
Strut Brown, John e49, **49**
Sunderland Street e**61**
Sutton Street e24, 25
Sydney Buildings f24, 52, 58; e**45**, 78, 89
Sydney College, *see* Bath (Proprietary) College
Sydney Gardens f8, **9**, 46, 51, 55, 63, 69;
    e19, 23, 24, **24**, 43, 44, 45, 46, 54, 61, 70
Sydney House (Hotel) e23, 33, 61
Sydney Mews e**34**
Sydney Place f**47**; e23, **23**, 33, **34**, 76, 81, 88
Sydney Road f8; e**19**

Sydney, Viscount, *see* Townsend, Thomas
Sydney Wharf f29, 50-56, **50-57**, 58, **60**, **61**, 62, 63,
    66; e47, 70
Sydney Wharf Road f8

Tasker, John e35
Teasdale, William f16
Telford, Thomas e87-88
Terry Farm e**13**
Theatre Tavern, The e63
Thimble Mill f64
Thompson, William e49
Thorne family f29
Thorpe, Thomas f**11**, 44
Thrale, Mr and Mrs f45
Titley, Jacob f12
Townsend, Thomas, Viscount Sydney e23
Trussler, Reverend Dr John f30, 47
Tucker, Mr f51
Tunstall, James e56
Tutton, William f84
Tylee, Miss f**81**, **83**

Undercliffe f69
Union Workhouse, Midford Road e22
University of Bath f53, 59, **61**; e18
Upper Great Pulteney Street e72
Usher, Archbishop f83

Vane, Harry George e81, **81**
Vane, William Henry and family e24, 25, **25**, 60
Vaughan, John and family f53, 54, 55, 73-74;
    e42, 57, **57**
Vauxhall Gradens, London f78; e45
Vellore Cottage e70-71, **70-71**
Vellore House e71, **71**

Vellore Lane f10; e70-71, **70-71**
Victoria Infants' School f78, 86; e57, **57**, **59**, 60, **92**
Villa Fields f33, 38, 43, 47, 48, **48**;
    e17, 28, 65, 70, 80-86, **81**, **82**, **84**, **86**, 89
Villa Fields Road e82, 84
Villa Place f**36**, 39, **39**, 41; e82
Vine Cottages f85
Vulcan House e69

Walcot f15, 21, 31, 32; e37, 44
Walker, Thomas e47
Warminster Road f69; e**39**
Weatherley, Frederick Edward and Miriam e51
Weedon, George e46
West, John f14
Westgate Street e35
Wherewell f8
White, David e35, 36
White, Henry e31
Whitehall Stairs f15
Whiting, Ernest e79-80
Whitings Motor Garage e69
Wiche/Wicke (Bathwick) f8, 10, 11, 12
Widcombe f15, 64, 78; e7, 12, 22, 43, 87, 88, 89
Wilkinson, Charles Hunnings e44
Wills, Miss Helen e61
Windsor Castle, The e70
Windsor Cottage e70, **70**
Windsor Terrace f49, **49**
Withers, Mr e11
Wood, John f6
Woodbine Cottage f67, **68**
Woodclose e7, **7**
Woodiwiss, Councillor e73
Wren, Sir Christopher f27
Wren, Sophia f27

Additional Bibliography

Meg Hamilton, *St. John's by the Fire Station*, privately published Bath, 1983

Terry Hardick, *The History of the Bath Boating Station*, Terry Hardick in association with
    Millstream Books, Bath, 2005

Paul Hardy & William Lowndes, *Profile of A City*, Redcliffe Press, Bristol, 1984

R.E.M. Peach, *Bath Old & New*, Simpkin, Marshall, London, 1886

Reverend Richard Prentis, *The Parish Church of St. Mary the Virgin, Bathwick*, privately
    published Bath, 1973

Edwin Smith, Olive Cook and Graham Hutton, *English Parish Churches*, Thames and
    Hudson, London, 1976

Barbara Stone, *Bath Millennium: The Christian Movement 973-1973*, privately published
    Bath, 1973

New Universal Encyclopaedia, Vols. 7 and 8, The Educational Book Company, London,
    n.d.

Introduction by Michael Rowe

Text by
Sheila Edwards, Terry Hardick, David Mitchell,
Robin Sales, Peter and Edith Wallis

Edited by Peter and Edith Wallis

Contributors

Vince Baughan, Krys Dodge, Mirella Keyford, Iris Law, Jack and Mary Sparrow
and other members of the Bathwick Local History Society

Acknowledgements

The authors wish to thank all those involved in the production of this book
and in particular the following for the support and use of their resources:
Mike Chapman
Andrew Ellis
Gill Huggins
Reverend David Prothero, Rector of Bathwick
Michael Rowe
John Wroughton
The Bath Chronicle
Bath Central Library
Colin Johnston and Lucy Powell of Bath Record Office
The Bath at Work Museum
Victoria Art Gallery

This publication was partly funded by
Voluntary Sector Funding for Small Groups,
B&NES Council Planning Services

Every effort has been made to obtain permission for the
reproduction of all illustrations used; our apologies for any oversight.